BLACK CAT PUBLISHING/IMANINATION

Nation: Uncaged

An Afro-Creole Perspective Poetry Collective From New Orleans

Darlene Marie Spears

This is dedicated to a phenomenal woman of integrity, dedication, wisdom, and courage. Thank you for inspiring me to be a voice in this world.

"…PEOPLE WILL NEVER FORGET HOW YOU MADE THEM FEEL."

MAYA ANGELOU

"LOOK IN THE MIRROR EACH DAY AND BE GRATEFUL THAT YOU CAN STAND, THINK CLEARLY, AND RECOGNIZE YOURSELF."

DARLENA MARIE SPEARS

TABLE OF CONTENTS

My Perspective...God is the author of my life.

I was born Darlene Marie Spears, but my momma called me Darlena. If I could not write, I would probably go completely insane. My life has been a colorful and diverse canvas of sunshine and rain. I began painting pictures with words as early as I can remember. As an English major, I studied, hoping to be approved by the academic world and acquire a better command of the English language. I spent my senior year serving as Editor-In-Chief at Southern University, and was inducted into Who's Who Amongst American College Students. I was formally employed in a myriad of professions, from public relations to waitressing, to acquire a formal education. To my dismay, the murder of a very close friend prompted my decision to relocate to New York. Prior to earning my degree, I attended Ben Franklin High School, the New Orleans Center for Creative Arts, Berkeley High in California, and Eleanor McMain Magnet, in New Orleans. While residing on the west coast during my teen years, I grew fond of the prominent voices of hip hop, which had become a mainstream voice of urban, conscious African Americans, who were blatantly expressing feelings of discontent; regarding racism, discrimination, lack of opportunities, and any social ills that plagued and festered in their communities. By my early twenties, ripe with rejection and anger, I was spiritually inclined to join the hip hop movement of free speech. Hip Hop ushered in beautiful and ugly truths about urban experiences without chasers, and the rap artists that I met were writers and entrepreneurs who had a message relative to their perspectives and experiences. My premier song in the early 90's, "I Ain't Goin' Out Like That", protested police brutality of African American males in American society in the 1970's and 80's. I was angry and outspoken by this time. Moreover, I had grown addicted to rapping because of the artistic freedom it welcomed in its niche. My entourage of three, including myself, was mentored and told that if we performed enough shows someone would discover us and sign us to a major label. We toured with local acts in cramped vehicles to do shows for $50.00, sometimes as far as Lafayette, Louisiana, or at the historic ILA dance hall located on Claiborne Ave. Performing as Imani X, I felt validated and well received, signing autographs in tiny country towns, or after packing a crowd in local high school gymnasiums. It was not until I subsequently moved to New York, was rendered homeless at the age of 25, due to a failed living arrangement, that I ever felt like a struggling artist. In no way did this hinder me from getting up the next morning and walking in front of the offices of Forty acres and a mule Film works as I had planned to do the day before. I have never told a single soul this until now, but the whole world changed to me that awful night. Determined to arrive by this time, I was convinced that life expects us to grow, like a weed, not always in the most desirable conditions. I never lost my way and was still focused on my dream. My living situation was inconsequential to me and what I wanted, or what I had designated as my destination. Moreover, I just shifted to automatic pilot; survival mode. One incident can dramatically change your perspective forever about everything. My family became my journal of poems and songs, and I was too busy entertaining my dream. Determined and focused each morning, I walked past the offices of 40 acres every single day, hoping to be discovered by Spike Lee. I was clad in cross colors clothing, a baseball cap, and my demo tape in the back pocket of my jeans. I felt invincible. Employment was a necessity, therefore, after living here and there with friends, I was hired as a teacher at P.S. 270 elementary in Brooklyn, New York and enrolled into Columbia University. Grateful and ecstatic upon receiving my first check, I immediately secured an apartment in the artistic Fort Green community in Brooklyn, which was conveniently in walking distance to Mr. Lee's offices. Initially, I started teaching to secure housing, however, all of the children in my class at P.S. 270 eventually became my own. Thus, my love for children was born and sewn into my dreams. My school was located at 241

Emerson place in Brooklyn, New York directly across the street from public housing and my students were composed of a diverse ethnic makeup. By this time, Crack cocaine had swept through every major metropolitan city, stressing and challenging the core of its urban population to its social and economic limitations. Mr. Lee's offices were less than a mile away, therefore, I was still able to walk by on my way home from work each day. Executive producer, Monty Ross, former vice president of 40 acres, finally saw and heard me after Joi Lee invited me into the building to share my demo tape with him. He ultimately signed me to his newly founded record label, Nu Wave records. As a performance artist for 7 years, I became a regular on the poetry scene in Brooklyn. Alcohol had become my demon that I was fighting constantly. Meanwhile, I was appointed to the New York city board of education's early childhood commission in New York for exemplary teaching skills around the same time. A domestic violence incident altered the course of my life, and I was temporarily derailed from my path. I decided to return to the big easy to heal and rejuvenate physically and spiritually. My vice principal, Ann Morrison invited me to live with her until I healed, but I declined. I will never forget her gesture of concern or kindness. Prior to my return, I was contracted to perform as a spoken word artist on an album entitled, "Miles 2 go", a tribute to Miles Davis, by the late mark Ledford in 1997, as Imani. Honestly, by this time I felt exhausted, and homesick. After returning home, I started attending the church of a high school friend, Bishop Darryl Brister, got saved at beacon light Ministries, married, gave birth to three children, and became a homeschool mom by the age of thirty. Growing up in the gumbo city, New Orleans, Louisiana, and residing in Hollygrove, located in the 17th voting district of New Orleans, molded me to be observant at all times of my surroundings and to protect what truly matters, self-respect. Uptown was always intoxicating with the sounds and smells of life. I studied piano and flute in my formative years, but my favorite instruments were the plastic buckets that my brother, his friends, and I manufactured beats on, imitating the marching bands we had seen at Mardi Gras. I studied ballet in books and practiced balancing and walking on metal fences. Cultural commerce in my community was contingent upon neighbors who were entrepreneurs that were generations skilled in cleaning, sewing, tutoring, music lessons, carpentry, painting, plumbing, catering, cooking, and auto mechanics. Every ward was a city within a city, with its own set of customs and beliefs, always seeming to compete with one another regarding sports, music, and anything one could fathom. Many places in the early 1970's in New Orleans strongly unwelcomed black people's business. Opened did not always imply welcomed. Black people knew where they were welcomed. Moreover, there were no white only signs, but you knew which neighborhood not to wander into, especially at night. It is no wonder that you could find someone to manufacture, fix, mend, or lead you to whatever you needed around the corner or down the street. We shopped at an exclusive children's boutique called Haase's on Oak Street for special occasions, because Mr. Haase's boutique welcomed black business. Oretha Castle Haley was the street that thrived with black owned businesses. As a child, I assumed my dad knew everyone in the city because he seemed to know one of each type of person really well. My father preached to me about working hard to accomplish goals in life. My dad would correct my speech constantly, and on the porch I would practice my colloquialism, and sing songs I knew that I shouldn't. My father was a strict disciplinarian, but we could always rely on our mom to allow exploration and discovery. We did not attend or belong to a religious organization, so most of my early religious teachings came from posters that I read in public places, assuming that the prophets were beautiful poets of long ago. All my life I have been indifferent to what people believe, but instead, have paid great attention to how they have treated me. In Hollygrove, gardens in backyards overflowing with fresh greens were not uncommon. Oaks and various fruit trees were scattered. The neighborhood lesbian's beautiful rosebuds bloomed each spring like clockwork on fences like they were climbing the perfect trellis, and I was always too eager to help her pick them. Life was alive and in season. I was the youngest of five, and in the melting summers after rigorous house chores, I would sit on my front porch and sip on a frozen cup and bask in the sounds and smells floating in the air. House parties on Fridays welcomed everyone and networking was inevitable. Politicians frequented parties at my house because my dad loved to discuss and address the issues and concerns of the community. Being sheltered at an early age, meant you could not leave the front porch, but I had a view to every imaginable scenario from this vantage point to love found, love lost, and love ignored. My neighborhood was full of the most colorful characters who believed in free speech and exercised it freely. Everybody spoke their minds and did not trust the police, who only came too late or after madness and death. I recall the time that a kid was raped and how quickly conversations ensued like a hornet's nest. One thing I am sure of is that most of the people in my neighborhood hated child molesters. A survivor of early molestation, I recall being afraid to tell for fear of what would happen to the accused. The small front porch in front of my shotgun house each day always mirrored something that was visually stimulating and I could not wait to finish my household chores and take a front row seat on the edge of the bottom step and draw or write the prevailing mood or attitude of the day. Every day was filled with fistfuls of cuss words or sprinkles of greetings and pleasantries that were sometimes whispered, mumbled, or yelled. One steamy afternoon, a trunk of secrets bellowed into the air like fireworks shooting off into the night sky. There were days I would sneak and sit on the concrete near the gate in order to get a closer taste of, what I perceived as, life beyond the gate. In the south, being a porch girl meant you were not allowed to go anywhere, confined to an eight by ten slab.Little did I realize at that time, my prison had become my art studio and writer's lab.

Once in the heat of summer, when I was six years old, a kid from the neighborhood offered a lick of their fudge popsicle, and I gratuitously accepted, coiling my tongue through the fence to taste the forbidden treat. I remembered being whipped by my father, because he had forbade us from making purchases at the store, as well as ever eating any items that were purchased from there, because he said that its owners had not signed a petition to repair our neighborhood streets. We were proud homeowners and most of my friends' parents were also. My community was made up of hard working people and professionals at the core of its infrastructure. My dad was the community advocate that people called when they needed anything from a ride home from the local Winn Dixie, to assisting with getting someone released from jail. Everyone knew him for being soft spoken, intelligent, kind, and generous. I miss him dearly. The only time that I ever felt different or thought I was ever poor was when we left my community and relocated to Broadmoor, which was a middle class community on the other side of Carrollton. In New Orleans, people of color had its share of local heroes, all of whom, made contributions to the rich culture. Billy Boden, Mahalia Jackson, Louis Armstrong, Homer Plessy, Ernest N. Morial, Reverend Avery Alexander, Reverend Skip Alexander, Judge Revius Ortique, The Marsalis Family, The Mason Family, The Charbonnets, The Gambino and Mckenzie families, all made contributions to the rich social, political, and cultural climate of New Orleans. Before relocating, I thought Hollygrove was a nation, and leaving Paul Laurence Dunbar to reluctantly attend A.D. Crossman, which was located in midcity, was not my idea of upward mobility. After leaving, I had an epiphany that Hollygrove was not a nation, but an allegory in America that was symbolic of a small community, closed within a much larger infrastructure, competing for its independence and economic viability, like many small town communities today. In my new community, my world seemed to have shrunken, become marginal and compromised because my familiar had changed.

Invariably, I wrote more, feeling isolated from the sounds of life, and familiar faces that I was accustomed to seeing on a daily basis. I missed my next door neighbors playing Aretha Franklin and daddy and I dancing to Nat King Cole after cutting the lawn on Saturday afternoons. I missed the girl named Dion, and her many siblings that I played with who had existed a stone's throw away. I missed seeing Daphne Mitchell, an older girl who always walked past my house on her way to the store, who later became my college roommate at L.S.U. She would no longer brighten my day with her gracious white teeth and beautiful brown skin each time she saw me. No longer would I greet my favorite cousin Gregory, who I proudly knew was the cutest and smartest boy at my school. I had just won an art contest for creating a brochure for my school, which rendered me a popular artist amongst my peers in the first grade. I did not trust the hushed quiet of this new place, the whispered conversations, and the strange unsolicited stares of some of my neighbors. Giant private fences, "private property", and "do not enter" signs were everywhere. After reading every book we owned and joining a book club, I entertained myself daily with doodling, reading, and writing short stories, songs and letters. I ultimately moved into the attic because I considered it the most quiet and interesting place in my house and my neighborhood. There I could find solace in the privacy of just myself and my words and we could play together uninterrupted. Without a television, I had lots of dolls that I brought to life, creating my own THE YOUNG AND THE RESTLESS. In my adolescence, I grew curious about the world that existed beyond what was familiar, so I started sneaking out of my room at night and joy riding with older and popular crowds. By the time I was 15, I smoked cigarettes, had a Mohawk, was a wandering teen, who would frequent clubs downtown or anywhere young people were not carded. My peers were now of diverse races and middle to upper class kids whose parents were corporate. My acclimation on any social scene was easy because diversity, in my opinion, is a natural part of life that exists.

There were white people who resided in Hollygrove in the 1960's that were cultural anomalies, scattered here and there. We coexisted without strife to my knowledge. I was indoctrinated with the belief that racism is evil, and that the skin color of the perpetrator or the victim didn't matter. Racism had not been a stranger to me growing up, often times being called a black nigger bitch, spook, or heckled, for who knows what reason, whenever I left upper Carrollton. My mother was of a mixed race and I was accustomed to being stared at whenever my mom and I would leave Hollygrove on a shopping errand into Old Metairie. I hated trips to Mississippi because we had to bring a bucket, water, and toiletries in case anyone had to use the restroom on the way. For this reason, I think people of color who live in the deep South are unsung heroes of true tolerance. Both of my parents vehemently forbade the use of the word "nigger", or any language that they deemed defiled the human spirit. I was resolved as a child to have a great day as long as some random adult did not give me a mean dirty look, or call me a nigger. Moreover, some white people were known to easily offend by what they perceived as a wrong look or gesture, so I was taught to never stare at them. New Orleans had invisible, but real segregated lines and it was considered traditional, not racist, to live the way we did. Separate but equal is still prevalent in the minds of some in the south who remain loyal to regional customs and beliefs. However, I have witnessed in my lifetime, the divergence of culture and customs in New Orleans, especially after Katrina. I am convinced that children who exhibit racist behaviors are simply modeling what they have been predisposed to in their home environment. Every experience, pleasant or not, dares us to own it and learn something new from it. I also believe that we are all exactly where we are supposed to be in each moment that we live. You must decide where you want to go from exactly where you are and plan to arrive, "by any means necessary". Today, writing is my secret escape once my children are asleep. I practice meditation and yoga each morning and work on slaying personal demons in my life by writing and sketching. I am grateful to have another opportunity to spend another day with my loved ones. I find that I am most creative when our house is loud with silence in the early morning hours. Life is not perfect and friends and parties have become a thing of the past. Writing is a place of refuge that I go to that is my sweetest companion. Throughout my life, I have remarried my dreams and ocean sounds in seashells remind me always of better days. Writing has always been extremely cathartic for me, my means to vent, my vessel to some understanding, protest, or a quiet resolution inside of myself. I have been writing my thoughts down since I was 5 years old. Ironically, in 2011, when I resigned from teaching, it was the first time I had no plan. Once more, my survival instincts kicked in, so I scribbled, jotted, and juxtaposed my frustrations regarding the teaching profession. I wanted to express real issues and concerns with some levity, thus, my first screenplay "teacher's pet", (title of screenplay) was born. It took almost one year exactly to write, and since then, I have given birth to songs, poems, and screenplays, which are the children of my dreams. I encounter most of them while asleep. I assure you it is like a blessing and a curse. I have written as a ghostwriter for many years in New Orleans for close friends and family, and in spite of any financial or personal losses, relished every waking moment in it. My writing is a bold and colorful cultural blend of who I am and what I have been exposed to advertently, or inadvertently. Like an indigenous pot of gumbo that must have its main ingredient to keep its integrity, I have remained true to my key ingredients in my work; heart and soul. I still love to sing, dance, draw, and paint, as best I can, at this age of forty something. I would probably lose my mind if I could no longer transpose my thoughts in some decipherable way. The transference of my thoughts is an exercise too enjoyable to be referred to as a hobby. I truly believe that every living creature is a beautiful blessing and we are souls strung together that are a collective of the most intricate and detailed beauty that is not tangible. I pray that my words reach as many people on the planet and helps to bring us all closer together. We should all strive to think freely and respect others. I am of the opinion that compassion and empathy are emotions that require higher order thinking skills. I write every single day, and it has never felt like a task, or a job. My greatest accomplishment was becoming a mother, which was unplanned, and giving birth to three amazing human beings. I have died in this world and come back to life, physically and metaphorically. The most amazing lessons that I have learned is to believe in you, find joy in being gracious and humble and never claim or feel lost. Should you ever get distracted or delayed, you must find your way back to your path. Do not let anyone lead you to something or somewhere that you never planned, but if you do, leave like you came. You are in control of where you want to get to in this world and must decide early on who you are and where you are headed. Most importantly, always have a plan before you travel and keep praying, working, practicing, living, learning, and above all, loving without expectation. Forgiveness is the highest form of selfless love. None of us are perfect in any way. I hope you enjoy my work. I humbly appreciate your interest. Know that I have crawled, walked, stumbled, fallen, died, and came back to life to become the person that I am today. Fallible with a young spirit and an old soul, God fearing and knowing we all mirror the creator. I bare my heart and soul to you in the hopes that you will join me and become a part of a nation, uncaged, and think freely in the absence of racism, which is fear and insecurity.

MY CAGED BIRD

I KNOW WHY MY CAGED BIRD CAN'T SING…
SO, I'M GOING TO SET HIM FREE… LISTEN CLOSELY AS I TELL
YOU EVERYTHING…TOO LONG THAT BIRD HAS BEEN TRYING
TO JUS' SURVIVE AND EAT, AND I KEEP TELLING MYSELF THAT
I SHOULD JUS' LET IT BE…
BUT IF I DO, MY CAGED BIRD WILL DIE…A SLOW DEATH FROM
BETRAYAL AND LIES. HER CAGE IS HER OWN FEARS AND
INSECURITIES,
SHE NEEDS TO FREE HER STORY, HER OWN SONG, HER
POETRY…

SICK OF NIGGERS FROM EVERYWHERE

I AM SICK OF WHITE, YELLOW, BLACK, BROWN, RED NIGGERS
JUDGEMENTAL CHRISTIAN NIGGERS, UPPITY, LOW CLASS
SHADY NIGGERS.
FAKE, WANNA BE NIGGERS...
BACKSTABBING, ASS KISSING NIGGERS
NIGGERS WHO STEAL CREATIVITY
NIGGERS WHO HATE FREE SPEECH
NIGGER MINISTERS WHO DON'T PREACH
NIGGER TEACHERS WHO DON'T REACH
NIGGER POLITICIANS WHO ARE CAREER CRIMINALS
NIGGERS WHO HATE TO THINK
NIGGERS WHO HATE JAZZ, RAP, OR POETRY
NIGGERS WHO HATE FREE SPEECH
NIGGERS WHO BLAME "THE MAN" FOR THEIR EVERY
TRANSGRESSION
NIGGERS WHO CHOOSE NO PURPOSE OR DIRECTION

NIGGERS WHO QUIT ON THEMSELVES AND THEIR DREAMS
NIGGERS WHO THINK BEING BLACK MEANS NOT BEING ABLE
TO SPEAK
NIGGERS WHO PUT SOMEONE ELSE'S NAME ON ANOTHER
NIGGER'S WORK, PROFIT AND THEN TRY TO DESTROY A
NIGGER AND THEIR SEEDS...FOR SURVIVING SUCH NIGGER
TYRANNY
LIGHT SKINNED NIGGERS WHO HATE DARK SKINNED NIGGERS
DARK SKINNED NIGGERS WHO HATE LIGHT SKINNED NIGGERS.
NIGGERS WHO THINK LIGHT SKINNED AND DARK SKINNED
NIGGERS ARE DIFFERENT.

WHITE NIGGERS WHO HATE EVERYBODY THAT DOESN'T LOOK
LIKE THEM.

NIGGERS WHO BITE THE HAND OF THOSE THAT FEED THEM.
NIGGERS WHO HATE THE COLOR OF THE SKIN THAT THEY'RE IN
NIGGERS WHO LOVE DIVISION AND DISSENSION
NIGGERS WHO HATE TO SEE NIGGERS ORGANIZING
NIGGERS SCARED OF OTHER NIGGERS RISING

NIGGERS WHO HATE DREAMERS, THINKERS, AND
INSPIRATION
NIGGERS WHO HATE REVOLUTION, TRUTH, AND REVELATION.
NIGGERS WHO FEAR A FREE NATION.
YOU CAN CALL ME WHATEVER YOU WANT,
BUT I AM NOT A NIGGER!
NO MATTER WHAT YOU TAKE FROM ME, YOU CAN NEVER
MAKE ME YOUR NIGGER. BEING CALLED A NIGGER IS
OPTIONAL FOR THOSE WHO ALLOW ITS PRESENCE AND CAN
APPRECIATE ANY NUANCE OF NIGRETUDE, BUT REFUSE TO LIVE
IN IT...BEING CALLED ANYTHING OTHER THAN WHAT YOU
CHOOSE TO BE CALLED, SHOULD ALWAYS BE QUESTIONABLE...

WAR
WAR WAGED UNSEEN
HIDES BEHIND THE EYES OF MEN
CREEPS IN THE NIGHT
WHEN PEACE SLEEPS
TIES UP DREAMS
AND HANGS OUT
HOPE TO DRY
ON A LINE THAT IS DRENCHED
WITH COVETED SCHEMES
AGENDAS ARE LIKE CURSES
TO THOSE WHO PRAY
AND PAY THE PRICE...
FOES CLOSE OR FAR AWAY
AND THE WORLD TURNS
IN A SEMI CONSCIENCE
STATE OF PLACING BLAME...
IN BETWEEN WANTING
PROTECTION WITHOUT
ANY OBLIGATION OR
RESPONSIBILITY...
DETACHED FROM WAR
YET, WARRING WITH ITSELF.

OLD TROUBLE AGAIN

HERE COMES OLD TROUBLE, BOUT TO SHAKE THINGS UP.
TROUBLE IS GOOD WHEN THINGS ARE UNJUST.
TROUBLESHOOTING IS NEVER NECESSARY WHEN THINGS RUN
SMOOTHLY.
THERE IS TROUBLE EVERYWHERE IN THIS OLD WORLD YOU
SEE. SOMETIMES TROUBLEMAKERS ARE REALLY
PEOPLE WHO SIT IN, LISTEN, WALK RIGHT, TALK RIGHT, KISS
ASS, SURRENDER LAND, SURRENDER RIGHTS, GRIN
AND SMILE, BEND OVER BACKWARDS,
DANCE AND SING, WORK FOR LESS THAN MINIMUM WAGE,
TREATED LIKE A REFUGEE,
COMMEMORATED AS A SLAVE, SIT BACK AND WATCH YOU ACT
LIKE AN EVIL, DISRESPECTFUL BASTARD, WHILE WE TRY TO BE
DIPLOMATIC AND PRAGMATIC. ALL THESE YEARS, WHY
HAVEN'T YOU LEARNED YOUR LESSON? WHEN THINGS ARE
UNBALANCED…LOOK UP YONDER,
OLE' TROUBLE WENT AND GOT ACTIVE,
HERE THEY COME TOGETHER.

PAIN

PAIN IS IN THE PAGES THAT WE WRITE...
BLOODY MEMORIES, SCARS, FIGHTING FOR RIGHT...
PUT DOWNS, HAND ME DOWNS, BRAND NEW BETRAYAL,
PHONY SMILES, LOTS OF LIES, BODIES FOR SALE
SETTLING FOR A MOTHER'S SECOND HAND LOVE
A FATHER'S ABSENCE, OR NO FAMILY AT ALL.
SITTING ON THE BACK PORCH AND FED SCRAPS LIKE A DOG,
NURSING WHITE BABIES, NO MILK LEFT FOR YOUR OWN,
COWORKERS WHO DESPISE YOU BECAUSE YOU ARE
PASSIONATE ABOUT YOUR FIELD...
PAIN TOO FAT, TOO SKINNY, TOO FAKE, TOO REAL, TOO SHORT,
TOO LONG
MOVE TOO FAST PAIN, TOO LATE, OR TOO SLOW,
ALCOHOL, CIGARETTES, FILTHY HABITS...
IT COULD BE BEATEN UP, RAPED, MOLESTED AND ABUSED AND
SILENCED
WORDS STOLEN, POEMS AND SONGS SUNG BY OTHERS
MISUSED, MISHANDLED, UNUSED, OR TAKEN FOR GRANTED...
A SCRATCH, A FIST FULL OF WORDS
A STUMBLE, A FALL
A MISSED MOMENT OR PERSON...
A JEALOUS LOVER, OR EVIL ASS BROTHERS...
A BUCKET OF BROKEN PROMISES AND FADING DREAMS,
A DYSFUNCTIONAL FAMILY THAT YOU LOVE...
DISAPPOINTMENT, FRUSTRATION, A CULMINATION OF ALL OF
THE ABOVE
DANCE TOO MUCH, DRINK TOO MUCH, PARTY TOO MUCH
PAIN....
PILL POPPING, RESTLESS, AND WEARY PAIN...
BLAMEFUL, UNGRATEFUL CRYING SHAME PAIN...

IT COULD BE RICH, HOMELESS, BRILLIANT, FLUNKY PAIN...

OR RACIST, PHILANTHROPIST, MURDERER, NUN PAIN...
IT CAN BE ANGRY, FUNNY OR DENIED,
SHOW UP ON A WORLD STAGE, IGNORED, OR SOMBERLY CRIED
SCRIPTED, TWISTED, ARTICULATED, LOCKED UP, SET FREE, OR
LOST INSIDE.
USE YOUR PAIN TO GROW AND THRIVE.
LIFE BEGINS WHEN PAIN BECOMES A SHADOW,
IT MAY FOLLOW YOU FOREVER, BUT HAS NO POWER OVER YOU
WHATSOEVER.

PAIN

RELATIVE

DIVERSE

PEOPLE

HEAL

BY

CONVERSING

SILENCE

IS

NEVER

AN

OPTION

STAND IN LOVE...

HE WAS THE BOY SHE CALLED HER FRIEND.
SHE TUTORED HIM AND GAVE HIM HER INNOCENT HONEY
KISSES.
HE SAID HE WAS IN LOVE CUZ THEY WERE 14.

LATER...THEY BROKE UP LIKE A PIECE OF STRING...
CUT IN HALF BY LIFE'S WINDS..
THEY BECAME ENEMIES BECAUSE OF SO-CALLED FRIENDS...

COLLEGE TAUGHT HIM HOW TO GET HIGH ON HEROIN...
AND SHE WAS HIS HALFWAY HOUSE TO RECOVERING....

ONE NIGHT HE WENT DANCIN'...ONLY HE WAS WITH ANOTHER
WOMAN...
SHE SAW RED, AND THEN THE NEXT THING YOU KNOW, SHE
WAS SPRAYING' HIM...
WITH WHATEVER SOMEONE GAVE HER TO DRINK...AND
BEFORE ANYONE COULD BLINK...
HE DROPPED HER FROM HIS SPELL OFF A BALCONY FOUR
STORIES UP ABOVE...
SHE THEN DECIDED...
THAT SHE WOULD NEVER AGAIN FALL IN LOVE...

CATS AND DOGS

I ONCE SAW A DOG ROAMING THE STREETS…
WANDERING WITH NO MASTER…
PISSING ON EVERYTHING…
HE NEEDED A LEASH…
EVERYWHERE HE STOPPED, HE BARKED MADLY…
AND HE WOULD MOUNT AND HUMP ANYTHING…
I KEPT THINKING...
SOMEONE SHOULD HAVE TRAINED THIS DOG…
I WONDERED ABOUT HIS OFFSPRING…
WERE THEY AS WILD AS HE?
WAS HE ABANDONED,
OR DID HE BELONG TO A FAMILY?

SO, IF YOU GET A DOG…
MAKE SURE HE IS HOUSE TRAINED…
OR HE'LL JUST PISS ABOUT ANYWHERE ON JUST ABOUT
ANYTHING…
NOT TEACHING HIM DISCIPLINE,
GIVES HIM NO DIGNITY…
HE WILL VAINLY BASK IN HIS OWN STUPIDITY…
AND PLEASE KEEP YOUR DOG ON A LEASH…
PLEASE TEACH HIM HOW TO STAY, SIT…
AND FETCH WHATEVER YOU MAY REQUIRE OR NEED…
OTHERWISE, HE'LL RUN WILDLY IN WONTON DESTRUCTION OF
OTHER PEOPLE'S THINGS…
IF YOU GET HIM AS A PUPPY,
GIVE HIM SOME LOVE AND AFFECTION…
BUT MOST IMPORTANTLY, TRAIN HIM TO DO THE
NECESSARY…
TEACH HIM TO SERVE ONLY ONE MASTER…
HIS GREATEST GIFT SHOULD BE SECURITY AND PROTECTION…

AND SINCE I AM A CAT, I HAVE TO TELL YA...
I CAN SMELL A STRAY DOG A MILE AWAY...
HE IS ALWAYS THE ONE THAT WILL CHASE...
WHILE HIS MASTER IS TRYING TO EXPLAIN,
"HE JUST WANTS TO PLAY...
HE DOESN'T MEAN YOU ANY HARM..."
I WOULD RATHER BE ALONE...
HE ROAMS FROM HOUSE TO HOME,
PISSING AND SHITTING ON PEOPLE'S LAWNS...
AND PLEASE GET YOUR DOG NEUTERED JUST IN CASE HE RUNS
AWAY...
CUZ HE WILL MAKE MORE OF HIMSELF WITHOUT ANY
OBLIGATION OR ACCOUNTABILITY...
WILD DOGS RUN IN PACKS BECAUSE THEY ARE WEAK...
FOLLOWING THE HDIC... (HEAD DOG IN CHARGE)
THAT IS FULL OF FLEAS...
WHEN YOUR DOG RETURNS,
ALL DISGRUNTLED AND FLEA RIDDEN...
DON'T LET HIM EVER SLEEP
IN YOUR HOUSE AGAIN...
IF YOU LAY WITH HIM, YOU CAN EXPECT AN INFESTATION...
HE JUST WANTS TO BE FED
AND GIVEN A WARM PLACE TO SLEEP...
WHY WOULD YOU REWARD HIM
FOR HIS LACK OF LOYALTY?
I KNOW SOME DOGS, BUT I KEEP MY DISTANCE...
CUZ I DON'T LIKE FLEAS AND DON'T LIKE TO START HISSING...
I KNOW I AM NOT MISSING....
-
CUZ I NEVER SAW A CAT BE A WILD DOG'S BOSS...
I HAVE WARNED YOU...
SO PLEASE PAY ATTENTION...
A WILD DOG IS A SELFISH BEAST...

THERE ARE NO EXCEPTIONS...

YOU CAN TRY YOUR BEST TO HOUSE AND TRAIN HIM,
SPOIL HIM, CLEAN HIM UP, AND EVEN PRAY FOR HIM...

YOU CAN GIVE HIM WHAT YOU THINK HE WAS
ALWAYS MISSING...
IF HE DOES NOT KNOW HIS FATHER AND HAS NO RESPECT
FOR HIS MOTHER, I'M SORRY, BUT YOU CAN FORGET IT...
THE DAMAGE IS TOO GREAT FOR ONE SOUL TO BANDAGE...
BY THE TIME HE IS FINISHES, YOU WON'T RECOGNIZE
YOURSELF IN THE MIRROR...

YOU WILL BLEND INTO AN ABYSS OF APATHY AND MENTAL
POVERTY, SPEAK LIKE HIM, WALK LIKE HIM, AND COULD END
UP
HOMELESS...HE WILL GO AS FAR AS TO BLAME IT ON
CULTURE...

DOGMA

IF YOU ARE KIND TO A DOG, SHE WILL PROTECT YOU AND
HAPPILY REMAIN LOYAL.

IF YOU BEAT AND ABUSE HER, ONE DAY SHE MAY TIRE OF IT,
AND JUST EAT YOUR ASS ALIVE. BUT, DON'T EVER EXPECT
HUMANITY, WHEN YOU TEACH AND PREACH DOGMA, BUT
BEHAVE LIKE AN ANIMAL.

DON'T EXPECT HER TO FOLLOW YOU AND OBEY FOR THE REST
OF HER DAYS...

DON'T TEACH HER RELIGION TO MAKE HER YOUR SLAVE...

DON'T INDOCTRINATE HER CHILDREN TO DISRESPECT FROM
WHENCE THEY CAME...

DOGMA ENCOURAGES CONTRABAND AND SUBMISSION...
JUSTIFIES INDIGNATION AND HUMILIATION...

THE BITCH IN HER WILL EVENTUALLY PREVAIL,

ONLY GOD HIMSELF WILL PREVENT HER FROM BITING OFF HIS
HEAD...

SOME MEN USE DOGMA TO OPPRESS THE WOMEN THEY SAY
THEY LOVE...TRUTH IS, DOGMA LOVES NO ONE.

THE MIRROR

WHEN I WAS A CHILD I LOOKED INTO THE MIRROR AND SAW
MY BEAUTIFUL REFLECTION…
AS AN ADOLESCENT, I SAW MANY FLAWS AND HOPED FOR
CORRECTIONS…
AS AN ADULT, MY FALLIBLE, VULNERABLE PERFECTION.

TIME

THE ONLY TIME THAT MATTERS IS THE
TIME WE HAVE SPENT TOGETHER THAT
WAS PLEASANT AND CIVIL...
THE REST, A BLUR OF INFINITE BLUNDER AND
DARKNESS THAT HOPEFULLY WE GLEANED A
LESSON OR LEST WE PRAYED TO FORGET...
THE ONLY TIME THAT MAKES A DIFFERENCE IS THE
TIME WE CARED OR GAVE A DAMN ABOUT SOMEONE OR
SOMETHING,
BASKED IN SOME OPPORTUNITY OR REBELLED IN SOME
OBSESSION...
THE ONLY TIME THAT MATTERS ARE THE MOMENTS
THAT WE LAUGHED OR CRIED TOGETHER TO CELEBRATE
SOMETHING OR SOMEONE'S PASSING...
HELD EACH OTHER UNCONDITIONAL IN LOVE'S SUBMISSION
TIMELESS IS THE SILENCE, IN THE SECURITY OF TRUSTING THE
ENERGY BETWEEN US
WORDS UNSPOKEN, NO APOLOGIES, ONLY OUR HUMANITY
TRANSFIXED IN THE SPACE THAT DIVIDES US
EVERY MOMENT BETWEEN LIFE AND DEATH THAT IS
CHERISHED, BY ONE OR MILLIONS...

TIMELESS, ARE INFINITE MOMENTS SHARED OF PLEASURABLE
EMOTIONS AND EXPRESSIONS
MEMORABLE WORDS AND EVENTS THAT WE EMBELLISH
THE ONLY TIME THAT MATTERS IS EVERY MOMENT BETWEEN
LIFE AND DEATH...
AND EVERY PRAYER EVER PRAYED OR MEDITATED

FOR ALL OF US TO EVOLVE INTO SOMETHING WORTHY OF
BEING REMEMBERED

ANTS AND PEOPLE
ANTS BUILD COLONIES PROTECTING THEIR QUEEN,
WORKING TOGETHER DAILY, WITHOUT STRIFE AS A
FAMILY...
AND WE
SELFISHLY WALK ON AND DESTROY THEIR LIFE'S WORK,
THOUGHTLESSLY AND SELFISHLY...
WHO ARE WE TO
QUESTION, ANALYZE THE GRAVITY, AND DESTROY SUCH
DEDICATION AND CONSISTENCY OF A MINISCULE
REPRESENTATION OF UNITY?
PERHAPS IT IS THEY, WHO ARE NOT MINDLESS,
BUT WE...WHO ARE SELFISH
MACHINES THAT ARE INSATIABLE BEASTS

MY LIFE

MY LIFE HAS NOT BEEN A BOWL OF CHERRIES,
OR SUNSHINY DAYS,
BUT I WON'T COMPLAIN…
GLASSY WHITE CHIPPED SIDEWALKS
AND DRUNK DREAMS HUNG OUT TO DRY
DRIPPING ON A LINE…
CRYSTAL CHANDELIER TEARS,
 PEEPING TOMS AND BLACKENED EYES…
SPLINTERED KISSES AND LIES…
I SURVIVED…
MY LIFE AIN'T BEEN NO LEMONADE,
COOL SHADE,
MORE LIKE STEAMY NIGHTS AND FLIES,
KNIVES, LIKE BLADES OF GRASS
IN MY BACK…
BUT I CAN'T COMPLAIN
CUZ I'M STILL SANE…
WITH EACH LOSS, THERE IS SOMETHING
TO GAIN…
LOVING THE UGLY SIDE IS A BEAUTIFUL THING
WITH EACH TRUTH THERE IS FREEDOM.
 I NEVER BECAME WHAT HAPPENED TO ME,
MY LIFE ALWAYS HELD THE SAME MEANING.
YEAH, NOW YOU KNOW MY LIFE AIN'T BEEN NO LEMONADE,
BUT I HAVE LEARNED TO DRINK IT DOWN EASY IN THE COOL OF
SOME SHADE.
NO WORRIES, IS WHAT I ALWAYS SAY.

BLACK LOVE

BLACK LOVE

BLACK LOVE STRUTTING THROUGH WHAT USED TO BE HER
PROJECT…
WEARING HOT PINK FLAMINGO SHORTS, TALKING TO
EVERYBODY
ABOUT EVERYTHING AND NOTHING…
BLACK LOVE BEATING HER TIRED HANDS WILDLY AT THE
EMPTY AIR IN RAGE,
HER 16 YEAR OLD IS DEAD,
HER ELDEST LIVES IN A CAGE
SHE ALWAYS KNEW WHY HER HIGH YELLOW MOMMA
MADE HER KILL HER BLACK BABIES
SHE WANTED TO RESCUE HER FROM THE GHETTO TYRANNY
AND DRAMA
NOURISHMENT FOR THE MIND, BODY, AND SOUL…
1000 YEAR OLD SONG SANG OVER AND OVER AGAIN
WE SHALL OVERCOME, WE SHALL…
BECAUSE OF BLACK LOVE…
WOMEN CARRYING BABIES ON THEIR BACKS AND IN THEIR HIP
JOINTS,
THEIR PRIDE TUCKED SECURELY AWAY IN THEIR BACK
POCKETS…
WALKING TO CHURCH ON MELTED PAVEMENTS,
SITTING IN THE BACK PEW.
TRYING TO SEE BEYOND THE BIG PINK HAT WITH WHITE
FEATHERS,
WAITING ON AN EASTER BASKET AND A MIRACLE…
LADIES IN WHITE TIPTOED DOWN THE AISLE BIG AND
BEAUTIFUL
AS THE PREACHER SANG…
AMAZING GRACE….
HOW SWEET THE SOUND OF BLACK LOVE…

GHETTOS CAN KILL PROPHETS AND TRY TO MAKE SISTERS
FEEL LIKE SASSY WHORES FOR PROFIT
MEANWHILE, STREET CORNERS FILLED WITH HUSTLERS,
GAWKING AND HECKLING…
BEGGIN' AND SINGIN' THE BLUES,
LOST DREAMS, LOST THEIR MINDS,
KILLING MY LITTLE BROTHERS WITH A NINE…
LOST BLACK LOVE,
LOST BLACK LOVE.
MUSTY SHOTGUN HOUSES REEKING WITH THE SMELL OF
SWEET AND SWEATY BODIES
THAT SWAYED AND BOUNCED TO RAP MUSIC…
AS A BROTHER LEANED ON THE WALL DRINKING' OLD E…
REEFER DANCING IN THE AIR
BLACK LOVE WAS THERE…
BLACK LOVE WAS THERE.
SHE WAS STANDING IN THE CORNER WAITING TO EMERGE,
TO CARRY HER BEAUTIFUL BLACK FLAMINGO, SO BLACK AND
STRONG, EVEN THE NIGHT COULDN'T COVER HIS **DARKNESS**…
OR HIS **BEAUTY**,

BRING HIM TO HER THRONE AND MAKE HIM A KING AGAIN…
INTRODUCE HIM TO MAYA ANGELOU, ZORA NEALE
HURSTON…ALICE WALKER, MAYA ANGELOU.
LET NIKKI G. FREAK HIS MIND
HOW SWEET THE SOUND…
OF BLACK LOVE…
FROM PICKING COTTON IN THE FIELDS AND NURSING PRECIOUS
WHITE BABIES, CLEANING THE HOUSES OF OTHER LADIES,
CLOAKED IN BLACK IN THE FRONT OF COURTROOMS, QUIETLY
RUNNING HOSPITALS, CORPORATIONS, AND CLASSROOMS…

WRITING OR SINGING HER VISIONS, BEING LOVED AND HATED
ON THE STAGE AND SCREEN, THE FIRST LADY AND SOMETIMES
THE LOWEST PAID
HER CROWN SOMETIMES LACED WITH POISONS AND DRUGS...
BLACK LOVE SITTING ON THE BACK OF THE BUS OR IN A
LIMOUSINE...
OFTENTIMES FAITHFUL TO SAVING HER BROTHER MAN
MISSING MEALS TO FEED HER CHILDREN
TOO BROWN FOR HER YELLOW MOMMA TO
EVER SEE HER REAL BEAUTY
SCRUTINIZED AND ANALYZED IF HER BLACK
PRODUCES RED BABIES...
CAUGHT IN BETWEEN WHAT HER RELIGION SAYS AND BEING
LIBERATED...
LOVED, FEARED, AND SOMETIMES HATED FOR NO GOOD
REASON
PRAYING FOR HER SEASON...
SACRIFICING FOR HER BLACK JESUS...
FORGIVING AND NEVER BEING GIVEN GRACE...
STUDIED, ANALYZED, MOCKED AND CRITICIZED
BY THE ONES SHE SERVES...

WEARING BLOODY SHOES FROM DESIGNING PYRAMIDS
CARVING HER STORY AND HER PAIN AND HER LOVE ON HER
BODY IN HIEROGLYPHICS...
 IN THE HOPES THAT SOMEONE WILL
READ IT OR PAY ATTENTION...
IN THE HOPES THAT ANOTHER WOMAN NEVER GOES THROUGH
WHAT SHE HAS BEEN...
HUNTED FOR BEING OUTSPOKEN,
UNBROKEN BECAUSE SHE WAS CHOSEN...
BLACK LOVE WAITING FOR SOMETHING RED, BLACK, AND
GREEN

TO SWOOP DOWN AND LIFT HER UP,

SINGING SWING LOW, SWEET CHARIOT,
COMING FORTH... TO CARRY...AND TIME ...TIME KEEPS
PASSING ON BY...
BLACK LOVE PRAYING,
BLACK LOVE WAITING,
BLACK LOVE MEDITATING...

MY COUNTRY, I SHED TEARS FOR THEE
PART 1

LAND OF EXPLOITATION AND HYPOCRISY. WHEN WILL
FREEDOM TRULY RING ?
SOME OF YOUR CHILDREN WEPT WHEN MR. OBAMA WON:
THEIR WORST NIGHTMARE, BORN TO A WHITE WOMAN AND AN
AFRICAN,
LAND WHERE MY FOREFATHERS WERE HUNG, RAPED MOTHERS
AND EXECUTED SONS.

TOO MANY UNSUNG EMMETT TILLS AND TRAYVONS.
TERROR AND TYRANNY UNLEASHED MORE THAN 450 YEARS
ON US.

THROUGHOUT THE YEARS I HAVE WEPT AND TRIED TO DO
WHAT IS RIGHT
WATCHING YOU PERPETRATE GREED, DOMINATION, AND FEAR
IN THE NIGHT
YOU EXPECT ME TO SMILE, KEEP PROTOCOL AND TURN MY
CHEEK,
WHILE YOU KEEP SLAPPING ME IN MY FACE,
 I PRAY ON BENDED AND BLOODIED KNEE.
WHEN WILL JUSTICE TRULY RING?
NEW SLAVES, OLD GAMES, YOU VILIFY AND CRITICIZE,
CORPORATE THEFT AND CONSERVATIVE LIES,
YOU BORDER LAND LIKE YOU ARE A GOD.
FROM EVERY COUNTRYSIDE,
YET YOU ARE A LENDER'S DEMISE.
WHEN WILL TRUTH AND JUSTICE RING?

SOMETIMES YOU ACT LIKE AN EVIL STEP MOTHER, MY STEP KIN.
AND YET, WE COME FROM THE SAME GARDEN.

FROM EVERY LAND FROM WHENCE YOU CAME,
I KNOW YOU DIDN'T WRITE THAT SONG FOR ME

AND YET MY LOYALTY TO YOU BECKONS MY VOICE IN THE SONG,
HAD IT NOT BEEN FOR X, MLK, AND KENNEDY, WE WOULD HAVE USED THE GARVEY PLAN LONG AGO.
LET JUSTICE AND FREEDOM RING…
I HAVE MUMBLED AND HUMMED SIDE BY SIDE, LIE FOR LIE, LOSS FOR LOSS, GAIN FOR GAIN, AND NOT COMPLAINED

WHEN WILL FREEDOM TRULY RING?
LET FREEDOM, TRUTH, AND JUSTICE RING!!!

MY COUNTRY, I SHED TEARS FOR THEE
PART 2

SWEET LAND OF WHITE BREAD, MILK AND HARMONY
FILLED WITH MEMBERS OF THE TEA PARTY
LAND FILLED WITH IMMIGRANTS,
WHO FLED PERSECUTION AND TYRANNY

DAMN..., JUST LIKE THE ONES TODAY...
BUT, WE NEVER THOUGHT THEY WOULD EVER WANT TO
STAY...
WE WANTED THEM TO WORK LIKE NEW SLAVES
THEY ARE THE REASON FOR OUR PROBLEMS TODAY.
REMEMBER WHEN EVERYONE OWNED AT LEAST ONE BIG
NEGRO.
NOW I SEE THEM EVERYWHERE I GO.
A MAN CAN'T EVEN ENJOY A BASKETBALL
GAME
I WANT TO WATCH THEM PLAY, NOT SIT NEXT TO THEM...
WON'T SOMEONE PLEASE EXPLAIN HOW THINGS GOT SO OUT
OF BLOODY CONTROL
WHY WON'T THEY JUST LOCK THE BORDER'S DOORS
I CAN'T CONTROL ALL
THESE BROWN PEOPLE!
THE GOLDEN DAYS WERE SEPARATE BUT EQUAL,
WILL SOMEONE PLEASE EXPLAIN,
HOW THESE ALIENS KEEP GETTING IN?
FUCK FREEDOM MAN!
THE GOOD OLE DAYS WERE BEFORE YOU CAME
WE BOYS AIN'T COME HERE TO SHARE THIS LAND
THIS COUNTRY WAS BUILT BY THEM NOT FOR THEM

MY PEOPLE WERE HERE RIGHT AFTER INDIANS,
WE FOUGHT AND KILLED FOR THIS HERE LAND
WE WHITE MEN ARE WARRIORS AND CONQUERORS, IT IS IN
OUR DNA.
WHY CAN'T YOU YANKEES UNDERSTAND.
JUST BE HAPPY THAT YOU ARE FREE AND NO LONGER FARM MY
LAND.
WE GAVE YOU AFFIRMATIVE ACTION THEN YOU WANTED OUR
WOMEN.
WE TREATED YOU MUCH BETTER THAN THE INDIANS.
YOU ARE UNGRATEFUL BECAUSE WE WROTE THE
CONSTITUTION
WITHOUT YOU.
SWEET LAND OF LIBERTY AND JUSTICE,
LET FREEDOM RING ON JUST US THE WAY IT
WAS INTENDED IN THE BEGINNING.
IF YOU DO NOT LIKE THIS COUNTRY, WHY WON'T YOU JUST
LEAVE IT?
LET FREEDOM AND JUSTICE RING FOR ALL OF MY PEOPLE.

WHAT'S IN A VOICE?

IT CAN BE SILENT,
OR SPEAK A NEGATIVE OR A POSITIVE.
WHAT'S IN A WALK?
IT CAN BE INSECURE AND FRAGILE OR A SUMMER STROLL,
YET, EVERY HUMAN BODY CARRIES THE WEIGHT OF ITS SOUL.
WHAT'S IN A DREAM?
IT CAN BE HOPE, FAITH, HARD WORK, OR DETERMINATION,
THAT COULD BE CAGED, BLOCKED, WAITING, OR NOT YET
SEEN.
WALK TALL AND SPEAK SOFTLY ABOUT WHAT YOU TRULY
BELIEVE.
SO IMAGINE IT!
SPEAK IT!
WALK IT!
CREATE IT!
SHARE IT, AND SET IT FREE!
THERE IS GREAT POWER IN WHAT WE RELEASE.

I DARE YOU!

I DARE YOU TO SPEAK LOUDLY TO THE WORLD WITHIN
YOURSELF AND DEFINE WHO YOU ARE.
MINGLE WITH EVERYONE, BUT BE FOLLOWERS OF NONE.
BELIEVE IN YOURSELF AND KNOW THAT TRUE MANIFEST
DESTINY IS A SINGULAR JOURNEY.
GROW UP AND STOP BLAMING OTHERS!
BE WISE, KIND, AND HUMBLE SO THAT YOU CAN EMPATHIZE,
APPRECIATE, AND RESPECT OTHERS; REGARDLESS OF PERSON,
REGARDLESS OF EDUCATIONAL BACKGROUND, REGARDLESS
OF COLOR.
I DARE YOU!

WHO WE ARE

WHO WE ARE CORRELATES WITH OUR ABILITY TO PERCEIVE
AND APPRECIATE EVERY MINISCULE ELEMENT OF EVERY
LIVING THING THAT HAS BREATH.
PAYING ATTENTION TO LIFE ITSELF,
WHO WE ARE DICTATES HOW WE TREAT OTHERS, NOT
REHEARSED OR MOTIVATED BY MONEY.
FATHOM THAT WE ARE ONE CANVASS OF A COLLECTIVE
CONSCIENCE.
WE CHALLENGE YOU TO CREATE A SPACE WITHIN YOUR
HEART THAT IS PASSIONATE ABOUT LOVING AND GIVING,
WITHOUT ANY EXPECTATIONS OR EXCEPTIONS.
WE ARE ALL PURPOSEFUL ENERGY, BECKONING TO MAKE A
DIFFERENCE.
WE ARE KIND, LOYAL, AND STRONG INDIVIDUALS.

WE ALL HAVE PURPOSE AND DIVINE MISSIONS.
WHO WE ARE; AMERICANS, EUROPEANS, AFRICANS, MIDDLE
EASTERNERS, ASIANS, LATIN AMERICANS, WEST INDIANS,
RUSSIANS, ALL INDIVIDUALS OF HUMAN MATTER.

THANK YOU MS. WINFREY FOR GIVING US YEARS OF FREE
COUNSELING AND EXPOSING THIS COUNTRY'S GOOD , BAD,
AND UGLY.

ACT WHITE?

ACT WHITE?

HER DAUGHTER CAME HOME WHEN SHE WAS 11 AND ASKED,
"MOMMY, WHAT DOES IT MEAN TO ACT WHITE?"
HER MOTHER SAID, WITH A SMILE, HONEY CHILE,
THAT JUST MEANS YOU'RE IN THE DEEP SOUTH.
BLACK IS BAD AND WHITE IS WONDERFUL!

SHE LOOKED AT HER DAUGHTER AND SAID,
WHAT COLOR IS AN ACTION?
PLEASE DON'T ENTERTAIN SUCH BASELESS DISTRACTIONS,
ACT LIKE YOU LOVE YOURSELF!
THINK OF IT AS A BACKWARDS COMPLIMENT INSTEAD.
SOME COWER TO LIVING A LIFE TRAPPED BY COLOR
TOO BLACK , TOO WHITE ARE STEREOTYPES THAT DIVIDE US
SO, JUST SHAKE YOUR HEAD IF SOMEONE SAYS
THAT YOU ARE ACTING WHITE.
SOME HAVE BEEN TOLD WHITE IS RIGHT AND BLACK IS BAD
AND TREATED THAT WAY FOR
TOO MANY YEARS.
JUST BE YOURSELF AND
I PROMISE YOU THAT YOU WILL BE OKAY.

TOO MUCH

TOO FAT, TOO SKINNY, TOO SHORT, TOO TALL, TOO LOST, TO FOUND,

TOO BLACK, TOO WHITE, TOO GAY, TOO STRAIGHT, TO HAIRY, TOO BALD,

TOO, MEAN, TOO NICE, TOO SLOW TOO FAST,

TOO EARLY, TOO LATE, TOO HYPER, TOO LAZY, TOO SMART, TOO SIMPLE,

TOO CRAZY, TOO ARROGANT, TOO HYPOCRITICAL, TOO SINNER, TOO CHRISTIAN,

TOO SURREPTITIOUS, TOO OBVIOUS, TOO SIMPLE, TOO SICK, TOO WELL,

TOO LOUD, TOO SOFT, TOO TALENTED, TOO CREATIVE, TOO COCKY, TOO HUMBLE, TOO PSYCHIC, TOO GREEN, TOO TRUSTING, TOO FORGIVING, TOO OPTIMISTIC, TOO SPIRITUAL...TOO SOULFUL

TOO SPIRITUAL?

TOO SPIRITUAL?

TOO MUCH WENT TOO FAR.

REMEMBER

REMEMBER

REMEMBER THE TIMES WHEN BLACK WAS BEAUTIFUL
BROTHERS WERE PROTECTIVE OF THEIR SISTERS, MOTHERS,
AND DAUGHTERS.
REMEMBER WHEN POETS SAT IN DIMLY LIT ROOMS CROONING
THEIR WARES TO A JAZZ, OR HIP HOP TUNE.
PAINTERS GAVE BIRTH TO MARY AND JESUS IN 3D AND COLOR.
EVERYBODY WAS DIPPED IN HOLY WATER.
JAMES BROWN WAS SINGING "I'M BLACK AND I'M PROUD."
AND MOHAMMED ALI WAS OUR BOXER WORD CHAMPION AND
MALCOLM AND MARTIN WERE OUR SCHOLARS TO FOLLOW.
OLD AUNTS TAUGHT THEIR NIECES TO READ FACES AND
HANDS.
CULTURAL TREATS OF UNKNOWN CHEFS FROM
FAMILIAR KITCHENS MINGLED IN THE AIR
CHILDREN STILL CHANTED INDIAN SONGS WHILE JUMPING
ROPE. EVERY MUSICIAN WANTED TO MAKE IT LIKE LOUIS
ARMSTRONG, OR BE PART OF A BRASS BAND.

NOBODY CARED ABOUT WHO DIDN'T LIKE BLACK.
VOODOO HAPPENED TO BAD PEOPLE WHO BELIEVED AND
EVERYONE WAS NAMED AFTER MARIE.
WHO DOO WAS UNKNOWN.
OLD LADIES ON FRONT PORCHES WATCHED YOU
LIKE YOU WERE THEIR OWN.
        REMEMBER WHEN...
BLACK WAS A LIGHT THAT EVERYBODY
 WANTED TO SHINE IN.

CULTURE

HAVE YOU SEEN MY CULTURE?

HE IS RUNNING DOWN THE STREET.

HE HAS LEFT ME AND IS GOING TO SHACK UP ON THE OTHER
SIDE OF TOWN WITH SOMEBODY HE JUST MET.

CULTURE WILL COME BACK, AFTER BEING PARADED, AND
DRAGGED THROUGH

THE STREETS, SOLD OUT, AND BOUGHT INTO.

HE WILL BE RAGGEDY AND LOOK DIFFERENT.

I WILL HAVE TO MEND HIM…

AND NURSE HIM BACK TO WHOLE WITH SUPPORT AND SOUL…

IF YOU SEE MY CULTURE WITH SOMEONE ELSE,

I AM RESOLVED THAT HE IS TOO SWEET NOT TO SHARE. HE IS
PRECIOUS TO ME, SO

JUST PLEASE DON'T LET HIM FORGET WHO HE IS AND HOW HE
ARRIVED THERE.

MOVE ON UP!
MOVE ON UP TO A HIGHER PLACE
FIND YOUR HIGHER POWER
REST IN KNOWING THAT YOU
ARE A PERFECT PLAN
AND NOTHING IS BY ACCIDENT
EVERYTHING THAT HAPPENS
A LESSON OR A BLESSING
IF I COULD GIFT YOU SMILES
OPEN YOUR HEART TO SEE
YOUR BEAUTY
I WOULD
BENEATH THE SURFACE
WE ALL SHINE
BEACONS OF LIGHT
SHINING IN DARKNESS
COVERED IN GLORY
GRATITUDE IS WHAT MAKES
US GRACEFUL
SWANS IN THE DEPTHS OF STRUGGLE
DEEP WATERS AND STORMS
UNABLE TO BREAK THE CALM
THAT IS LAYERED IN LOVE
VALLEYS AND MOUNTAINS
PEAK AND RECEDE
WE FEAST FROM THE TREE
OF KNOWLEDGE
OR WALK ON SACRED WATERS
BUT HERE, EVERYONE IS THE SAME
FLAGS AND SYMBOLS GIVE
US A REASON TO
PART SEAS
BUT YOUR SAIL IS UNBROKEN

YOUR MASS IS YOUR UNCONQUERABLE
SOUL
YOUR SPIRIT IS THE WIND
THAT PREVAILS
ASCENDING AND DESCENDING ARE WE
TRUMPETS RESOUNDING
THE SONG OF VICTORY

ONCE YOU OVERCOME,
YOU WILL MOVE UP TO A HIGHER PLANE
TAKE YOUR PLACE RIGHTFULLY
RIGHT YOUR OWN WRONGS
FORGIVE AND FIGHT TO
LIVE IN A PEACE WITH EVERYONE
AND SING VICTORY
SWEET VICTORY SONGS

DREAMS ARE BORN TO LIVE...TO GIVE...A PERSPECTIVE...TO THE MINDS OF MANY, **THAT CAN CHARTER SOME UNSEEN OR UNKNOWN COLLECTIVE OR A FAMILIAR RECOLLECTION**

DREAMS

I HAD A DREAM,
A VISION IN MY SLEEP. MY HAIR HUNG
WILD, UNCOMBED, AND FREE…DANCED TO THE RHYTHM OF A
THOUSAND YEAR OLD SONG, IN A PLACE WHERE WE TRULY
BELONGED, IN A PLACE I COULD TRULY CALL HOME.
NO IGNORANCE, INSECURITY, OR POVERTY.
EVERYBODY WAS RICH IN EVERY IMAGINABLE WAY.
I HAD A DREAM…
GHETTOS WERE A THING OF THE PAST AND EVERYBODY
MOVED UP
AND LIVED AND ATE LIKE KINGS AND QUEENS…
I HAD A DREAM OF ECONOMIC PARITY…

IMAGINE

IMAGINE

IMAGINE A RAINBOW WITHOUT COLOR,
SUN WITHOUT RAYS, BIRDS WITHOUT WIN
IMAGINE BOOKS WITHOUT WORDS,
PEOPLE FACELESS, STARLESS SKIES
IMAGINE A MOTHER NEVER HEARING HER
BABY'S CRIES
MOREOVER, NEVER GIVING BIRTH
WOMB BECOMES TOMB
LIPS NEVER KISSED BY YOUR LOVER.
IMAGINE MUSIC WITHOUT MELODY,
THE ABSENCE OF LAUGHTER,
SLEEPLESS NIGHTS
 AND ENDLESS THUNDER
A FLOWER UNABLE TO BLOOM
OCEANS AND SEAS WITHOUT THE COLOR BLUE
IMAGINE DANCING WITH PAIN, SLEEPING WITH
DISAPPOINTMENT
MAKING LOVE TO REJECTION, FOUL PLAY, AND NEVER
TASTING SUCCESS OR PLEASURE.
NOW, YOU CAN IMAGINE WHAT IT'S LIKE
FOR SOME TO BE YOUNG, GIFTED, AND BLACK IN AMERICA.
IMAGINE THAT
CIRCLES CAN UNDERMINE YOUR SUCCESSES

TOO MELANATED TO BE CALLED JUS CREOLE

SEE HAIR WAVY, CURLY, AND SOMETIMES DRY, THICK AND HEALTHY.
SOMETIMES CULTURAL ANOMALIES WITHIN THEIR OWN CIRCLE OF FRIENDS.
MELANIN AGITATES SOME, SO SOMETIMES THEY ASSIMILATE IN.
CHAMELEONS IN THEIR OWN SKIN,
THEY DON'T MIND STANDING ALONE,
OR SITTING ON EITHER SIDE, STANDING FOR WHAT'S "RIGHT"
TOO BLACK, AND DEFINITELY NOT WHITE.
AFRO CREOLE BABIES
SMOOTH JAZZY, SASSY, MOCHA, CARAMEL, CHOCOLATE, VANILLA LADIES,
SEXY BROWN AND CARAMEL LATTE SOLDIERS AND HANDSOME BLUE BLACK AND RED DOCTORS, AND LAWYERS,
SWEET SUGAR MOMMAS, HUSTLERS,
POLITICIANS, AND ICY JAZZ MUSICIANS THAT DON'T BITE THEIR TONGUES
IF YOU SEE A LITTLE BROWN GIRL CHASING BIRDS, BECAUSE SHE WANTS THEM TO TEACH HER TO FLY FREE...
PLEASE REMEMBER ME AND BROWN PAPER BAG TESTS THAT PERPETRATED LIES AND DIVISION.
REMEMBER THE CREOLE MEN AND WOMEN OF DISTINCTION FROM NEW ORLEANS WHO MADE A DIFFERENCE.
THE REBELS OF FRENCHMEN STREET, THE "DUTCH", THOSE WHOM WE COULD NEVER FORGET...

HOW DARE YOU!

JUST WHEN I THOUGHT WE WERE THROUGH.
HERE YOU COME AGAIN, TAIL BETWEEN YOUR LEGS.
LIFE KICKED YOU IN YOUR ASS, WITH FORTY DOLLARS AND
MORE PROMISES…
YOU ENCOURAGE MY WRITING AND OPEN COVERS,
REFER ME TO ANOTHER GHOSTWRITER'S DUNGEON…
AND I AM YOUR FAITHFUL RETREAT TO WHAT IS REAL.
YEARS HAVE GONE BY AND I AM BEGINNING TO AGE.
SUPPORTING YOUR DREAMS AND LISTENING TO YOU
COMPLAIN ABOUT THE GAME.
HELP MAKE DADDY FEEL BETTER IS WHAT YOU ALWAYS SAY.
HOW DARE YOU SAY I SHOULD WAIT ON MY DREAM, UNTIL
THE KIDS ARE ALL GROWN,
HONEY CHILE, BY THEN I WILL BE GREY AND OLD.
I GAVE YOU ALL MY MONEY, MOREOVER,
ALL OF THE INSIDE OF MY THOUGHTS…
YOU AND YOUR CLICK BETRAYED MY ONLY TRUE LOVE
YOU LEFT ME STANDING IN THE MIDDLE OF MY LIFE, TWO
KIDS, MISSING THREE, SET ME UP WRITING SONGS FOR THE
DEVIL THAT WAS SENT STRAIGHT TO ME FROM GOD HIMSELF
AS A MINISTER MAN
SERENADED INTO SIN AND LIFE'S FORBIDDEN PLEASURES
I WAS LEFT STANDING WITH A HABIT YOU SUGGESTED,
A BUCKET OF BIBLE LESSONS, SOME SKIMPY DRESSES, AND NO
PAYCHECK …I WILL NOT APOLOGIZE FOR MY LOYALTY OR MY
TRANSGRESSIONS…
HARLOTS AND HUSTLERS COME UP TO FALSE WITNESS
AGAINST ME…
ERASE MY DESTINY AND BREAK MY SPIRIT.
A WOMAN SCORNED KNOWS NO FREEDOM IN THE GHETTO,

BUT YOU WILL NOT HAVE THE LAST WORD OR SING THE LAST
SONG IN THIS GHETTO MANIFESTO
YOU INTRODUCED ME TO A NEW WORLD OF SIN
WHEN I LET GO OF THE PAST, MY LIFE WILL BEGIN.
EVEN THOUGH SOMETIMES YOU'RE HERE,
DON'T GET THIS TWISTED,
FORGIVENESS IS TO BLAME,
CUZ COLD BODIES CAN GO INSANE, BUT I WOULD RATHER
BE ALONE THAN LOSE MY MIND IN THIS GANGSTER'S GAME.
HOW DARE YOU EVEN THINK YOU COULD EVER GET BACK INTO
MY HEART AGAIN! I REALIZE YOU NEVER DESERVED TO BE
THERE IN THE FIRST PLACE

MY PEOPLE

MY PEOPLE PRAY FOR ME
LAUGH WITH ME
SHARE WITH ME
LOVE ME FOR ME
NEVER STRIKE ME
HUSH ME
CRADLE ME
HUG ME
SMILE WHEN OUR EYES MEET
CRY TOGETHER WHEN WE WITNESS TRAGEDY
MY PEOPLE LOVE ME
AND I LOVE THEM
WHEREVER THEY MAY BE
MY PEOPLE ARE EVERYWHERE
IMPERFECT, FORGIVEN, DIFFERENT
GENUINE IN SPIRIT
GIVING IN THEIR LIVING
HUMBLE IN THEIR LOVING

DIG DEEP!

DIG DEEP!!

I NEED SOME SUN TO SHINE DOWN ON ME
I'VE BEEN IN THE SHADE TOO LONG
MY BODY IS COLD AND SHIVERING FROM LIES THAT LED TO
PEOPLE DOING ME WRONG
I NEED SOME SUN TO RAIN DOWN ON ME LIKE A RAGING, BUT
GENTLE STORM
I'M GOIN' DIG DEEP DOWN IN MYSELF IN THIS DARK PLACE.
I WILL DIE HERE IF I DON'T FIND ME SOME SUN,
PULL IT OUT, AND PUT IT ON.
I GOTTA DIG REAL DEEP INSIDE OF ME CUZ' I BEEN
RUNNIN' FROM MY PAIN FOR SO LONG.
WHEN I FIND MY SUN I AM GOING TO DIG DEEP, POUR AND
DRINK IT ALL UP UNTIL I AM GOOD AND FULL.

SPEAK!

SPEAK OF THE PAST,
SPEAK OF THE PRESENT,
SPEAK OF THE FUTURE,

WE MUST CONVERSE WITH ONE ANOTHER.
WE ARE AN ORAL CULTURE.
SO SPEAK TO YOUR SISTERS AND BROTHERS.
REMEMBER THE STRUGGLES,
ENCOURAGE ONE ANOTHER!
FREE SPEECH!
TAKE FREE SPEECH OUT OF YOUR TRUNK, DUST IT OFF AND
BRING IT UP!
DRESS IT UP OR DRESS IT DOWN!
PARADE IT, SING, IT WRITE, OR PLAY IT,
ALL AROUND TOWN.
THINK FREELY AND SPEAK!
WE MUST CONVERSE WITH ONE ANOTHER IN ORDER
TO PRESERVE OUR OWN CULTURE
LEST IT BE TRULY FORGOTTEN.

SO SPEAK OF YOUR FUTURE, PRESENT, AND PAST.
WRITE IT DOWN, SO THAT
IT CAN SPEAK GENERATIONS BACK.

EDUCATIONAL DILEMMA

HER SON CAME HOME FROM THE 6TH GRADE AND HUNG HIS
HEAD AND SAID,
"I HAVE A CONFESSION, MY TEACHER TOLD ME IN FRONT OF
THE WHOLE CLASS THAT I AM NOT GOING TO BE READY FOR
7TH GRADE, BECAUSE I LAUGHED DURING A LESSON."
SHE SHOOK HER HEAD AND SAID,
SHE IS OBVIOUSLY IN THE WRONG PROFESSION.

I WISH THERE WERE NO GHETTOS IN AMERICA ; NO POVERTY,
NO RACISM, NO CLASSISM, NO SEXISM, NO ENVY, NO GREED,
NO ECONOMIC STATUS...IMAGINE A WORLD WHERE ALL
PEOPLE TRULY MATTERED.

RECOVERY

HE WAS BIBLE TOTIN' TONGUE SWEARING PRODUCER MAN
WHO WAS A PREACHER
HE MADE GOD PROMISES AND SENT THE DEVIL TO PLAY WITH
HER CHILDREN...
SHE WAS A GHOST WRITER JUST TRYING TO MAKE HER FIRST
MILLION...
NEVER KNEW SNAKES COULD WEAR BOW TIES AND USE
SCRIPTURE…
TONGUE TWISTED REALITY WITH HYPNOSIS AND POTIONS
HE GAVE HER SMOKE STICKS SO SHE COULD FLOW MO BETTER,
WHILE MEN SAT AROUND LISTENING TO HER SPIT ANCIENT
WORDS FROM OLD SPIRITS TO MELODIES
MARKED HER CAR WITH FEDERAL FLAGS AND STICKERS
SHE LOOKED IN THE MIRROR ONE DAY AND HARDLY
RECOGNIZED THE SCARECROW SHADOW...
BY THEN SHE WAS SCARED TO RUN, CONFUSED AND WAS
WAITING ON GOD OR SOME CELEBRITY RESCUE TO HAPPEN
TO CUT HER CHECK AND CUT HER LOOSE…
HER REALITY SHOW, HER STUDIO, HER YOUTH, HAD BECOME
BURIED,
VIDEOS, PHOTOS, FAKE FRIENDS MARRIED...
SHE WAS RICH ALREADY IN HER SPIRIT FILLED WORLD
OF ALL THAT TRULY MATTERED…
ALL THE SONGS SHE HAD WRITTEN WERE DANCING ON THE
RADIO SOLO, WITHOUT HER IN THEIR ARMS
THEY TRIED TO LOCK HER AWAY AND THROW AWAY HER
DREAMS
TURN SECRETS INTO NIGHTMARES

FORGOT THAT HER FATHER TAUGHT HER TO THINK LIKE

A BOSS MAN, HOLD HER CARD UNTIL SHE NEEDED IT
EMPTY SHE LEFT, TO FIND HERSELF, AND NEW SONGS AND
SCREENPLAYS TO MAKE LOVE TO
 THAT NO ONE WOULD HUSTLE OUT OF HER,
MAKE BELIEVE WITH CASKET AND RING THAT THEY LOVED
HER
 BECAUSE THIS TIME SHE WOULD CARRY THEM TO THE
MARKET WHERE DEALS WERE MADE,
 AND SHE WOULD SIT AT THE TABLE WHERE CHECKS ARE
WRITTEN.
GROWN WOMEN SHOULD NEVER BE HUSHED LIKE CHILDREN.
HER COLLEGE DEGREE WAS NO MATCH FOR THE LEVEL OF
STREET THAT SHE HAD MET
YEARS OF LIFE EXPERIENCE HAD NOT DEALT THE CARDS
THAT WERE BEING DEALT TO THOSE IN HER INNER CIRCLE
SHE WAS DAMNED NEAR TURNED INSIDE OUT BY LIFE LESSONS
THE WORSE FEELING IS TO HEAR LAUGHTER AIMED AT YOU
MINISTER MAN, PRODUCER, LOVER, WOULD NOT TRAP OR
TRICK HER INTO WRITING AND SINGING ON CONSIGNMENT,
 OR TRADE WORDS FOR BACK RUBS OR AFFECTION.
WHO WOULD BELIEVE HER WHEN PAPER TRAILS LIE AND
RUMORS TAKE FLIGHT BECAUSE MONEY CAN MAKE GOOD BAD
AND BAD SEEM GOOD ALL DAY LONG NO MATTER WHERE YOU
LIVE.
HER CHILDREN ARE BLINDED BY WHAT COULD HAVE BEEN AND
WHAT TRULY IS
TRUTH IS…
LATE NIGHTS WRITING SACRIFICED TIME THAT SHE COULD
NEVER REPLACE
NEW FRIENDS USHER IN TO DIVIDE AND CONQUER WHAT IS
LEFT OF FAMILY
AND THE WORLD TURNS ON AN AXIS OF WHO THE NEXT
SUCKER IS, THE NEXT MONEY MAKER, THE NEXT BLOCK TAKER

AND HER CROWN STAYS SECURELY ABOVE THE FRAY BECAUSE
SHE ALREADY KNOWS THE WORLD CAN BUY YOUR SUCCESSES
AND YOUR FAILURES AND TURN YOUR LIFE INSIDE OUT AND
REGURGITATE YOUR DREAMS THROUGH PORTALS WHILE WE
WATCH OTHERS DIE RIGHT IN FRONT OF US ON CORNERS OR
FAR PLACES ON THE NEWS THANKING GOD THAT WE HAVE A
BED TO SLEEP IN
THEY MADE HER WISH TO LIVE IN THE GHETTO WHERE
YOU CAN SEE YOUR ENEMY COMING
 PEN AND PAPER CANNOT CHANGE WHAT ANCESTORS AND
ANGELS WRITE FOR EACH ONE OF US IN OUR TIME
LABELS CANNOT REWRITE YOUR BIRTHRIGHT
OR CHANGE YOUR GOD'S MIND.
DESTINY CAN NEVER BE DENIED.
HER RECOVERY IS THE BIGGEST LESSON, THE BIGGEST LIE, THE
ONLY LISTEN IN A CIRCLE OF BIG TIMERS AND BIG MOUTHS,
WHO PRACTICED BECOMING BOUGIE TO WATCH HER DEMISE
THE GREATEST SHOW ON EARTH WAS NOT WHAT SHE
ENVISIONED
BUT EACH NIGHT SHE DREAMED HER MIND WAS A MISSION
TO SHARE WITH ALL CREATION
HER FAITH WAS AN ANOMALY, AFTER ALL THE
DISAPPOINTMENT
HER JOY AND PEACE WAS UNFATHOMABLE TO THOSE WHO
WERE SUNKEN INTO DEPRESSING OTHERS WITH LABELS
MEDICATION WAS OUT OF THE QUESTION FOR HER, BECAUSE
MEDITATION HAD BROUGHT HER TO A PLACE OF
UNCONDITIONAL LOVE
AND HER SPIRIT WAS DEAFENED TO
LOUD LIES THAT WALK STRAIGHT AND WEAR SUITS AND TIES
AND HIDE BEHIND THE MONEY SHE MADE THEM AND DRIVE
NICE CARS AND TAKE VACATIONS…
HOPING THAT SHE WON'T MAKE IT

THE UNCONSCIOUS FOLLOWERS OF ALL OF NOTHING,
ARE THE BIGGEST PAWNS AND VICTIMS OF A MEDIA FRENZY
NEGATIVE ATTENTION CREATES AN AUDIENCE OF THOSE WHO
HAVE NO COMPASSION BECAUSE THEY HAVE DECIDED THAT
THEIR LIFE IS NOT INTERESTING ENOUGH TO TUNE INTO .
IN HER RECOVERY THAT NEVER WAS GOD'S PLAN...BUT
MAN'S...
A FEW GOT TO KNOW HER WELL ENOUGH TO GET HER TO
TASTE TRUSTINGLY, THE POISON THAT WAS MADE TO DESTROY
HER BEAUTIFUL MIND ONCE THEY HAD SOLD HER SPIRIT SPEAK
EASY
IN BACK ROOMS AND FAKE STUDIOS..
HER BLACK HEART IS UNBREAKABLE IN LOVE WITH HER
MAKER
RECOVERY, SHE BELIEVES IN
SHE NEVER KNEW A LOVE LIKE THIS BEFORE
LOSSES ARE PREPARATION FOR VICTORY IF YOU DO NOT
SUCCUMB TO THEM
 TO SURVIVE HERE SHE HAS TO LIVE HER TESTIMONY
BREATHE HER TESTIMONY
BECOME HER OWN STORY
RECOVER DAILY BY BEING GREATER THAN ANY DERAILING
WITH EACH BREATH, CLIMBING EACH STEP
ON AN UNPREDICTABLE AND SOMETIMES SHAKY TRACK
FALLING IS NEVER AN OPTION, HANGING ON TO WHAT
MATTERS IS ALL THAT IS AT STAKE
KEEPING YOUR SOUL FROM SHATTERING
NEVER ALLOWING THE ICE YOU FEEL TO FREEZE YOUR BRAIN
KEEPING YOUR HEART PROTECTED
LIFE MAKES A MOCKERY OF PLANNING.
RECOVER DAILY!
RECOVERY IS THE ONLY TRUE METHOD OF SURVIVAL IN THIS
REALM!

SHE WENT BACK TO WHERE HIP HOP IN NEW ORLEANS IS BORN
DON BARTHELEMEW'S STUDIO HAD HER PRESCRIPTION
HIS MUSIC WAS HER THERAPY
AND THE BEAT PLAYS ON..
THE BEAT PLAYS ON

SPIRITS SPEAK
WHEN TONGUES FAIL
SPIRITS SPEAK TRUTHS
THAT SHUDDER MAN
WEAK ONES PAIL
STRONG ONES PREVAIL
SAINTS AND SINNERS
FALL ON THEIR KNEES TO PRAY
WHEN ANCIENT SPIRITS SPEAK
THROUGH MAN
ON MOUNTAINTOP
OR PULPIT
IN TINY TOWN THROUGH PORTAL
OR FORGOTTEN GRAVE
SPIRITS SPEAK
FREEING SLAVES
TRAPPED BETWEEN TIME
HEALING SPLINTERED LIVES
AND GIVING PEACE TO SHADES
SPIRITS SPEAK THROUGH ALL OF MEN
DANTE'S DOOR OR HEAVEN SENT
PROTECTING THE INNOCENT
KARMA SMOTHERING THE UNJUST
IF ONLY THEY WOULD SIT STILL TO LISTEN
AND DISCERN WHICH SPIRITS TO TRUST

PSALMS OF MARIE
IT DOESN'T MATTER
IT DOESN'T MATTER WHAT THEY TOOK OR WHAT THEY STOLE..
AS LONG AS YOU HOLD ONTO TO YOUR SOUL…
YOU CAN TRY AGAIN…
IT DOESN'T MATTER WHAT THEY SAY OR WHAT YOU DID,
I KNOW THE TRUTH
AND I SEE YOU
DRY YOUR EYES MY FRIEND
AND I WAS THINKING YOU AND I
COULD SOMEDAY GO
TO A PLACE WHERE ONLY DREAMERS KNOW
WE CAN FLY AGAIN
IF WE TRY AGAIN
IT DOESN'T MATTER IF YOU NEVER GET THE GOLD
AS LONG AS YOU HOLD ONTO YOUR SOUL
IT'S YOUR TIME TO WIN
YOU CAN FLY MY FRIEND

NEW ORLEANS
IF I NEVER FALL IN LOVE
I'LL THANK MY LUCKY STARS ABOVE
JUS' REMEMBER I LOVE YOU
IF I NEVER CRUISE OR SAIL
OR MY LIFE ENDS UP IN A FAIRYTALE
JUS' REMEMBER I LOVE YOU
I WAS BORN IN NEW ORLEANS
STRAIGHT OUTTA THE 17
JUS' REMEMBER I LOVE YOU
WHEN YOU GET TO NEW ORLEANS
 HOPE YOU ALL THINK OF ME
JUS' REMEMBER I LOVE YOU!!!

IF
IF ONLY THEY DID NOT PRICK HER IN HER SLEEP
PUT POTION IN HER DRINK
LIE TO HER ABOUT HER PAYMENT
CASH CHECKS BEHIND HER BACK
THREATEN HER WITH HER PAST OF
INNOCENCE AND LACK OF INHIBITION
THEIR ATTEMPTED COMMITTAL WAS HER
REALITY SHOW IN A SEA OF BETRAYAL
IF ONLY EAGLES FLEW FROM MOUNTAINS TO
SHOW HER THE WAY OUT OF THE CAVE THAT
THEY DUG TO ENSLAVE
HER TALENT
CAPTURE THE KNAVE OF FEAR
DIG OUT THEIR LYING EYES WITH ITS TALONS
IF ONLY THEY HAD NOT CONSPIRED
TO FORCE HER INTO RETIREMENT
INTO POVERTY OR
SWOON HER TO DEATH
STRANGLING HER GIFTS
PHOTOGRAPHING HER BARE
BENEATH PROMISES
AND SHEATHS OF NIGHTMARES
REMOVING THE SOLES OF HER SHOES
STRIPPING HER OF WARDROBE
AND CONSTANTLY UNDRESSING HER CHARACTER
WITH ENGAGEMENT TO ALTER
THAT NEVER HAPPENS
STAGED COMPANIONS AND FAKE LAUGHTER
WHISPERS OF SLANDER
AND RUMORS TO COVERED BASES
AND HIDDEN TRACKS THAT ALL LEAD TO HER
BEING STABBED IN THE BACK

SEMICIRCLE SHE PRAYS TO GOD FOR
FORGIVENESS FOR HER NAIVETY, THE OTHER HALF SHE
REPENTS TO ONLY DATE SELF
IF ONLY THEY HAD NOT FORGOTTEN THAT SHE,
LIKE A SPIDER, GREW UP IN A WEB OF LIES AND SAW
DISAPPOINTMENT IN MOTHER'S EYES, WENT TO AN INFANT'S
FUNERAL AT FIFTEEN AND BY SIXTEEN HAD ALREADY
LOST TWINS. IF ONLY THEY HAD KNOWN THAT SHE
HAD SEEN URBAN ANGELS LAMENT AND WORE BRUISES
LIKE A SECOND SKIN AND WATCHED THE MOST TALENTED
DANCERS AND POETS ASCEND TO HEAVEN'S GATE TOO SOON
TO LAMENT
IF ONLY SHE HAD KNOWN THAT EVIL COMES, EVEN MORE,
FOR THOSE WHO ARE UNSELFISH AND HONORABLE
 MORE SO, THAN FOR THOSE WHO ARE PRETENTIOUS AND
PIOUS
BECAUSE EVIL SEEKS TO DESTROY THE MOST BEAUTIFUL

A SONG OF PRAISE

SING A SONG
SING A SONG OF VICTORY
SING OUT LOUD
GIVE PRAISE
GIVE THANKS
FOR SIMPLY BEING AWAKE

GHOST WRITERS BEWARE

THEY KEPT SAYING SHE WAS DIFFERENT
DID HER MARY JANE BECAUSE SHE WAS SWEETER
TOOK HER KINDNESS AND RESPECT FOR WEAKNESS
SOME KNEW HER AS QUEEN SUGAR
SENT WHORES WITH BIG SMILES AND NINJAS WITH FAKE KISSES
YEARS WENT BY AS THEY CAME AND WENT BACK AND FORTH
TO THE BIG CITY
ALL HITS NO MISSES
SHE IS NOT YOUR WRITER SLAVE
SHE IS NOT YOUR JEZEBEL
SHE NEVER WANTED TO BE A STUDIO MISSUS'
CROSSED HER TEXT AND TONGUE IN THE END
CASHED CHECKS AND DID NOT INVITE HER TO DINE OUT OR IN
CALLED HER PAUL, LISTENED TO HER LIKE Z. HURSTON,
AND SAID SHE WOULD END UP LIKE BILLIE IF SHE DID NOT
LISTEN
WANTED HER TO STAY ON THEIR STUDIO PLANTATION
WHERE WRITERS WORK FOR THEIR SO CALLED PEOPLE,
WRITING FOR CANNED GOODS, WHILE THEIR KIDS
KEEP PRAYING AND GOING TO THE CHURCH HOUSE
LIKE AN OLD NEGRO SPIRITUAL,
LONG FORGOTTEN, KICKED OUT NICELY
ARE WE REALLY IN THE TWO THOUSANDS?
HER CHILDREN WATCH AND WONDER WHAT HAPPENED
TOO YOUNG AND TOO DISTRACTED
WISHING MOMMA HAD HER OLD JOB BACK,
OR DADDY RENEWS HER CONTRACT
SO THAT SHE COULD JUST WORK IN DAYLIGHT LIKE
BEFORE THE STUDIO HOOK UP ON THE HUSH,
EVERYBODY PLAYS THEIR PART IN KEEPING HER IN HER PLACE,
EXCEPT HER SISTER WHO IS ALWAYS THROWN OFF GUARD

POVERTY BACKLASH; DEMOLISHED HER CREDIT,
INFILTRATED HER DWELLING, GANGSTERS AND CRUMB
SNATCHERS PLACE INSURANCE BETS...
WHEN SHE SLEEPS THEY ENTER TO PRICK HER WITH POISONS
SHE PRAYS NO WEAPON FORMED AGAINST ME
SHALL PROSPER...
THIS IS SOME CAIN AND ABLE BULLSHIT
SOME JAILHOUSE SHIT,
SOME UNDERGROUND DEVILMENT,
THEY PUT LIZARDS IN HER GARDEN
TO EAT AWAY AT THE SEEDS SHE SPAWNED AND PLANTED
GHOST WRITER, ONLY SOMETHING GREATER THAN HERSELF
COULD EVER HAVE RESURRECTED ANY OF THIS,
IN THE RUBBLE SHE HAD TO FIND HER QUEENNESS...
AND ALL SHE CARED ABOUT WAS FEEDING HER BABIES WITH
PEN AND PAPER...
SHE CANNOT INTELLECTUALIZE BETRAYAL WITH A HASHTAG
THAT IS REAL ENOUGH TO EXPRESS WHAT SHE HAS SEEN OR
HER ANGER
SHE PRAYS FORGIVENESS OF THEM AS THEY ACCUSE HER OF
BEING UNSTABLE
HER BARE HANDS PUT FOOD ON THEIR TABLE
SOME MADE MONEY, SOME GOT DRUGS CARS AND HOUSES,
SOME WERE OFFERED PLEA BARGAINS...
TO KEEP HER UNDER THE TABLE AND SILENCED
A LITTLE MONEY IN A SMALL CITY CAN FORGO CORRUPTION
MIRRORS CANNOT HIDE THEIR FACES WHEN THEY READ THESE
WORDS, LETTERS ARE UNBREAKABLE WRITTEN IN VERSE
GOD WILL NOT ERASE WHAT THEY HAVE DONE
A GENERATIONAL CURSE IS WHAT SHE WAS THINKING
BUT THEY ARE HER KINFOLK AND SO CALLED FRIENDS OF
FRIENDS...

SO, SHE PRAYS THAT GOD WILL LET THEM LIVE TO SEE HER
SOAR
CRUMB SNATCHERS AND PIGEONS LEFT ALONE TO FIGHT OVER
CRUMBS AND SPOILS
 LET THEM WATCH HER MAKE GUMBO OUT OF SNAKES AND
ROCKS THROWN IN HER PATH…
OUTLIVE HER ENEMIES BY SPEAKING ANCIENT SCRIPTURE TO
LIFE
WATCH HER KISS CROSSES UNBROKEN ON CHURCH STEPS
LIGHT CANDLES AND SAY NOVENAS TO SAINTS AND
ANCESTORS
DANCE IN HER OLD AGE TO THE SOUND OF CONTENTMENT
MAKE LOVE TO DISAPPOINTMENT AND DINE WITH SOLACE
HUMBLE TO LINES CROSSED AND ABUSE BURIED…
FORGIVE AND TURN THE OTHER CHEEK, BECAUSE
SHE KNOWS THAT THE GREATEST REVENGE IS SUCCESS
AND KARMA, WELL SHE IS A HOT WHORE OF A MESS.

HOLLYGROVE
HOLLYGROVE WAS A NEIGHBORHOOD
WHERE OLD LADIES WERE EVERYONE'S
GRANDPARENTS…
OAK TREES AND FRUIT TREES SCATTERED
CHILDREN PLAYED HOPSCOTCH, DODGEBALL,
MARBLES, AND JACKS…
MOST PEOPLE WENT TO CHURCH ON SUNDAYS.
SOME TO ST. JOHN'S, ST. JOAN OF ARC, OR
THEY WERE BAPTIST
 EVERYBODY ALWAYS SAID GOOD AFTERNOON
AND GOOD MORNING IN PASSING
WE ALL DREAMED OF BECOMING SOMETHING POWERFUL AND
AWESOME SO THAT WE COULD BUY A MANSION
LIKE ON THE OTHER SIDE OF TOWN FOR OUR PARENTS

BLACK WRITERS IN THE SOUTH

BLACK WRITERS IN THE SOUTH CAN BE HUNTED LIKE
BOBCATS IN THE NORTH BY NEXT OF KIN
OR BROTHERS WHO SAY
THEY LOVE YOU TO DEATH
PLANTATION WOES, INTELLECTUAL PIMPS AND
BOURGIE WHORES
IN THE NEW WORLD ORDER
TECHNOLOGY AND GREENSCREEN
MAKES A SISTER AN EASY TARGET
FOR THE NEW SLAVE CATCHERS
THE NEW BLACK MARKET
OF THE DREAM DEFERRED
BLACK LYRICS, LIKE GOLD WATER,
GIVES THEM THE LIFE THEY ALWAYS WANTED
PIMPS HIM OUT TO BE THE MAN HE
FEELS HE NEVER WAS, OR
COULD BE TO HIS SONS AND DAUGHTERS
OBLIVIOUS TO IT ALL, AND FOCUSED ON
THE MONETARY BLACK POWER
THE BLACK BOUNTY HUNTERS
LAY CLOSE AND WAIT TILL
NIGHTFALL...
TO CREEP IN AND STEAL
YOUR FREEDOM PAPERS
YOUR WORKS OF ART
SONGS, POETRY, OR ANYTHING YOU HAVE WRITTEN
A NIGHTMARE THAT IS RARE
BUT LIKE MOST SOUTHERN POLICE TALES
NO ONE SEES OR TELLS
AS NEARBY POCKETS FATTEN
NO WITNESS PROTECTION

LIES ARE TWISTED LIKE A
ROPE AROUND YOUR NECK
SISTERS AIN'T NO SISTERS
SOMETIMES, YELLOW, BROWN, OR BLACK,
CUZ SHE NEEDS
TO GET HERS AND THAT IS ALL
THAT MATTERS...
OFF PROBATION OR OFF TO NEW PROPERTY IS A
MOTIVATING
FACTOR...
THAT CHILLS HER CONSCIENCE
A NEW OFFICE SATIATES HER PALETTE
AND EVERY SUNDAY SHE PRAYS FOR
FORGIVENESS...
IN THESE STATELY MATTERS
ALL OF HER BLACKNESS COULD NOT
MAKE A BLACK WRITER'S LIFE MATTER
SHE EXPECTS SECONDS...
AT THE EXPENSE OF OBEYING HER MASTER
AN ALL STAR CAST OF WANNABES
AND AVERAGE JOES AND LEFT OVER TOMS FROM
SEGREGATION...
WHO JOINED IN TO TAKE PART OF THE FINAL ACT
OF PONTIOUS PILOT AND THE WELL LADY
BROTHERS DREAM OF LIVING LIKE
WHAT HE DEEMS IS THE WHITE MAN'S WORLD...
AND EVERYONE IN HER PATH IS FOR SALE,
EXCEPT HER SISTER WHO IS FAITHFUL
WITH CANDLES, OILS, AND PRAYERS
AND HER DAUGHTER AND SONS WHO ARE
HER BLESSINGS GOD GAVE
BROWN SKIN IS THE LEAST EXPENSIVE
ORNAMENT DANGLING ON THE FAMILY TREE

AND SHE HAS COME TO KNOW IT ALL TOO WELL
MOMMA'S BLUE EYES CAN'T SAVE HER
FROM THE DEPTHS OF INDUSTRY HELL,
BLACKMAIL, OR BLACKBALL, OH WELL...
FINGERPRINTS TAKEN, SWAPPED, OR STOLEN
UNTIL SHE PRAYS NO WEAPON FORMED AGAINST ME...
GOD KEPT HER FROM THE CHAINS THAT
SHACKLE CREATIVE HANDS
AND CAGE THE GIFTED MINDS
WHO NONCONFORM TO THE IGNORANCE AND HATRED
THAT IS WONTON
WITH NO PURPOSE, JUSTIFYING UNGODLY PERSECUTION
PAID PRODUCERS AND DIRECTORS COME AND GO...
SHE SLEEPS WITH ONE EYE OPENED AND ONE EYE CLOSED
CLINGING TO HER LAST HAND WRITTEN NOTES
WONDERING IF SHE COULD RUN FAR AWAY TO
ESCAPE THE INJUSTICE THAT MAKES NO SENSE
TO THOSE UNAFFECTED IN HER PRESENCE
LOCK HER WORK INSIDE HER HEART AND THROW AWAY
THE KEY
ONLY GOD CAN GIVE HER COMFORT IN THIS PILE OF MESS
TEMPTED, ROBBED, STRIPPED OF LOVE AND THEN
ABANDONED
PHOTOGRAPHED LIKE A CELEBRITY OR AN EXOTIC
ANIMAL
AND NOBODY GETS WHAT IS OBVIOUS
SEDUCED BY JUDAS', WHO WERE MALE
PROSTITUTES AT BEST
SLAVE CATCHERS ARE THE INDUSTRY'S FINEST
A TEN YEAR PLAN TO SEEK HER DEMISE
SUIT AND TIE
UNDERESTIMATED HER UNBREAKABLE LINES
SHE WROTE THOSE LINES

THEY DID NOT EXPECT HER TO REACH FOR A ROSARY
OR VEST HERSELF IN ANGELS, SAINTS AND ANCESTORS'
STORIES
SINNERS CAME, UNPLANNED AND UNSCRIPTED TO DEFEND
HER
GOD HIMSELF, STEPPED IN, TO SAY ENOUGH WAS ENOUGH
RESTORING HER SPIRIT AND LIFTING HER UP
BOGUS CRITICS AND HUSHED PRAYERS
AMONGST EAR HUSTLERS, FAKE FRIENDS,
COPY CATS, HAS BEENS, AND WASHED UP PLAYERS
WHO SAID SHE DESERVED ALL OF IT...
BECAUSE WORDS ARE FOR SALE ON THE BLACK MARKET
IN THE SOUTH...
FREEDOM OF SPEECH IS PRICELESS, SILENCE NOONE
FEAR CANNOT RUN DESTINY, NOR, CAN IT SABOTAGE
OR CONQUER TRUTHS FROM SOUL
FAILURE IS NEVER AN OPTION
GOD'S PLAN IS WHAT FOLLOWS
BUT SHE WILL BE DAMNED IF SHE DOES NOT BECOME SPEAK
UP AND SPEAK LOUD IN SHAKE DOWN WATERS
THEY SAY BLACK WRITERS ARE BIG MOUTHS
WHO THINK THEY ARE TOO MUCH
SOME RAPPERS, SOME POETS, SOME JOURNALISTS...
SOME ALL OF THE ABOVE
SHE WONDERS OFTEN TIMES, IF BLACK WRITERS
EVER TRULY MATTERED WHEN THEY WERE ALIVE
TO THOSE CLOSEST,
THOSE WHO PROFITTED?
SHE IS JUST GRATEFUL TO HAVE SOME BALANCE AND
STILL ACKNOWLEDGE A
HIGHER POWER.
HER TATTOO IS A SYMBOL OF HER STORY
HER STRUGGLE...

THIS IS IN REMEMBRANCE OF BLACK WRITERS THAT
HAVE PASSED ON OR HAVE FALLEN.

WRITE YOUR STORY
LIVE IN GLORY
BASK IN THE KNOWING
BE UMBREAKABLE
LOVE LIKE NEVER BEFORE
SPIRITS WILL SPEAK
IN YEARS TO COME
FALLEN ANGELS
WILL RISE ONCE MORE
FLOWERS GROW IN THORNS
SUN WILL POUR WHEN DARKNESS
COMES
FAITH WILL CARRY US TO JOURNEY ON
WORDS ON PAGES CAN MAKE
US GRATEFUL THAT IT WAS
 NOT ABOUT US
YOUR STORY IS WRITTEN
BEFORE YOU LIVE IT
SO KNOW THAT SEASONS
GOOD OR BAD
LESSONS OR BLESSINGS
MAKE US WHO WE ARE

FOR WHOM THE SOUL TOLLS
A SACRED MOMENT
OF BLISSFUL SONGS
THAT REST BESIDE HER
AND DANCES CHEEK TO CHEEK
A SEMICIRCLE OF WAKING MOMENTS
THE OTHER HALF ASLEEP
DREAMS LIKE DE JA VU
ONLY HEAVEN SCENT
OR NIGHTMARES FORECAST
AN IMMINENT DESCENT
A GLANCE THROUGH A
TIMELESS GLASS
STAINED LIKE CHURCH WINDOWS
UNBELIEVABLE SOUNDS OF JOY
STEEP FROM SPIRITUAL TEMPLES
FOR WHOM THE HONOR BEARS
THE WEIGHT OF DISBELIEVERS
PRAYS THE PRAYER OF
DIFFERENT, BUT EQUAL
OH LORD, THE ONLY PLEASURE I
HAVE KNOWN HAS BEEN SCRIBE
IF NOT ON PAPER, STONE
IF NOT MY OWN, THE CONCERNS OF SOME
WHO SPEAK, BUT ARE UNWILLING TO
RECORD
LOVE OR STENCH OF NIGH
CONSUMED WITH CREATING
PICTURES WITH PEN AND PAPER
BUT WHEN SIMPLIFIED,
MISCONSTRUED AS SIMPLISTIC
AUDIENCE AND CRITIC NEVER SATISFIED
WHAT WORK DO I HAVE

TO SHOW?
EXCEPT THE TOIL
OF MY BROW WRITTEN DOWN,
WORDS CANNOT CROWN MY DAUGHTER
OR ADORN MY SONS,
OR GIVE LIFE TO THE UNBORN…
OH CURSED THING THAT I DO,
THAT IS AN INVISIBLE BLESSING
THAT ENTRAPS ME AND MONOPOLIZES
MY TIME, SABOTEUR OF RELATIONSHIPS…
FOR WHOM IS THIS SELFISHNESS
JUSTIFIABLE THROUGH A PEN
OR THE MIND'S EYE A COMPANION?
A PRIVATE OBSESSION MOURNFULLY
FOR SOME PENNIES ON THE DOLLAR,
PUBLICLY SHOWCASED OR EXPLOITED…
BETRAYED, BEWILDERED, I RETREAT TO
MY HANDS FOR FORGIVENESS, REDEMPTION
AND FAVOR…
ASKING GOD TO GUIDE MY PEN ON PAPER,
NEVER EXILING THIS WRETCHED THING,
AN INFINITE LOVE AND HATE RELATIONSHIP…
THIS ALBATROSS ENVIED AND DESIRED,
BRINGS BUZZARDS AND FLIES
 PLUCKING AND TAKING AWAY PIECES OF MIND, TIME,
OR JUST BEING A MEDDLING NUISANCE,
ENTERTAINING OR DISRESPECTFUL DISPOSITIONS…
WHAT EGO LIES ALONGSIDE WHAT IS ALWAYS
SCRUTINIZED OR QUESTIONABLE TO THOSE
WHO CANNOT COMPREHEND HOW WORDS BECOME
SUSTENANCE AND MEDICINE?
WORDS REPLACE LOVERS AND MEMORIALIZE
MEMORIES AND CONFRONT ENEMIES

AND EXPOSE EVILS
SOME WORDS MAKE US LAUGH
CRY, OR SEE OURSELVES,
RIGHT OURSELVES,
OR DENY WHO WE ARE...
WORDS PROTECT CHILDREN AND
SING PRAISES AND HOLD PRAYERS
WORDS HEAL SCARS,
BREAK CURSES AND
FORGIVE...

LOVE
LOVE WAS STANDING IN THE MIDDLE
WAITING TO BE BORN
CRADLED BY ITS MOTHER'S WOMB
SILENT IN THE DARK
PERHAPS IT IS AN ALLEGORY
THAT THE WORLD WAITS TO
COMPREHEND
IN THE ABSENCE OF INSECURITY
IN THE ABSENCE OF FEAR
IN THE ABSENCE OF RELIGION
IN THE ABSENCE OF POLITICS
LOVE WAS CONCEIVED
THE IMMACULATE CONCEPTION
INDEED IT IS PERFECTION
IN THE ABSENCE OF HUMANKIND
SOMETHING TO BE DESIRED
SOMETHING TO BE SPAWNED
ITS SEED WAS PLANTED
LONG BEFORE YOU OR I
IT IS THE MELODY IN SONG
THE SUN IN SKY
THE UNEXPECTED RAIN SHOWER
THE FULL MOON'S DELIGHT
A LOVER'S SOFT KISS
THE WIND CARESSING CHEEK
ON STEAMY NIGHT
BREEZES AND BUTTERFLIES
THAT MAKE LOVE TO THE
WEARY AND DREAMS THAT
NEVER DIE
LOVE REMINDS US OF ETERNITY
AN INFINITE SHADOW THAT LOOMS

IN DARKNESS
THAT BLANKETS NAKEDNESS
THAT COMFORTS
THE UNRECONCILED

JAZZ MUSIC
CRYSTAL CLEAR MOANING
REJOICING CALLING
IRISH JIGS AND A SLAVE'S VIOLIN
MADE LOVE
NEGRO SPIRITUALS TAKE FLIGHT
FROM UNDERGROUND
RAILROADS AND TRAINS
SING IN SYNCOPATION
SPEAK EASY IN FREEDOM SONGS
OR DANCE WITH THE DEVIL TO CANDLELIGHT
GOSPEL REMINDS US NOT TO CARE
BODIN AND ARMSTRONG
LAUGHED AND CRIED TOGETHER
SLEEPING BLUES CAME AND RESCUED THE
LONEY
WEARY ESCAPE SOUNDS LIKE
MILES ROARING LIKE A LION
SERENE AND SMOOTH MADE
COLTRANE COOL COMMON
ELLINGTON MADE
ELEGANT BECOME BLACK
WHEN TUXEDOS HELD HORNS
ARROGANCE IS EXPECTED
GIFTS ETERNAL
SORROW RESPECTED
MAHALIA AND ELLA
WAILED IN THE MELODY
DURING TIMES OF CIVIL
MADNESS
AND BILLE FELT THE WRATH
INSIDE OF HER GOD BLESS
PRAYERS, CONFESSIONS,

AND REBELLIONS
IN A STANZA DANCE
CAB CALLOWAY MADE
THEM SPEAK BACK
AND LENA'S BEAUTY
WAS UNSURPASSED
CHARLIE PARKER'S
BIRD LAND, A SACRED PLACE
LEADING TO MR. MARSALIS' GARDEN
SOWING SEEDS OF YESTERDAYS AND
TOMORROWS
MR. LEE MADE IMAGES A MUSICAL CHOIR
SCREECHING SIRENS SIGNAL
CIVIL DISOBEDIENCE
DRUMS COMMAND US TO DANCE TOGETHER
AND PIANOS LAMENT AND EMBRACE THE INEVITABLE
THE TRUMPET REMINDS US THAT
THERE WILL ALWAYS BE A STRUGGLE
AND THE GUITAR CALMS THE STORM
AND USHERS IN ROCKS THAT ROLL
LITTLE RICHARD AND SAMMY DAVIS WERE BORN
DOWN IN NEW ORLEANS
DON BARTHOLEMEW AND TOUSSANT
ADDED FRENCH AND GUMBO
AND THE ROOTS OF JAZZ
GROW ON RAPPING, CROONING,
BOUNCING IN THE STREETS
OF NEW ORLEANS AND THE WORLD...
HATS OFF TO THE TRUE MASTERS

To The Younger Generation: Cycle Breaker

POLICE BRUTALITY IS A HORRID THING
I FEEL MOTHER'S CRIES FOR YOUNG BLACK MEN
WOMEN AND MEN ABUSED BY FRIENDS,
IS A NEGLIGENT NIGHTMARE TOO OFTEN
HUSHED INTO A PIT OF SHAME
VICTIM BURDENED IN THE COMMUNITY
WITH BEING LABELED NAÏVE OR CRAZY
FOR ALLOWING TRESSPASSING
THEFT CAN STEAL ONES INNOCENCE
AND REMOVE ALL TRUST FROM
CONSCIOUS THOUGHTS
RAPE VICTIMS WHO NEVER
SEQUESTER THEIR PERPETRATORS
FOR FEAR OF SCRUTINY
LIVE A LIFE OF HUMBLE FORGIVENESS
TO AVOID JUDGEMENT AND GOING INSANE
ELDER ABUSE IS PURE EVIL
AND CHILD ABUSE IS A SIGN
OF INSTABILITY
THE BLOOD OF STRUGGLE
HAS BEEN DRAWN
FALLEN ANGELS SPEAK FROM
THE PAST TO REMIND US TO
BE STRONG AND UNDAUNTED
WHEN TROUBLED TIMES COME
IN MY LIFETIME, I HAVE HEARD
OF TRAGEDIES AND BORE WITNESS TO
PEOPLE FAILING IN THEIR HUMANITY
BRUTALITY COMMITTED BY ANYONE
IS AN UNNECESSARY ACT OF VIOLENCE
I URGE YOU TO REMEMBER THOSE
WHO HAVE SACRIFICED BEFORE YOU

SO THAT YOU COULD LIVE
GROW AND EVOLVE IN SOCIETY
I URGE YOU TO PRAY
AND KNOW THAT GOD IS IN CONTROL
BEFORE YOU PICK UP A CAUSE
I IMPLORE YOU TO LIVE
AS THE FUTURE OF HOPE
BE GRATEFUL AND HUMBLE
RESPECT YOURSELF AND OTHERS
I DARE YOU TO BE SUPERNATURAL
AND ACCOMPLISH SOMETHING SPECIAL
AND LIVE LIKE YOU ONLY HAVE ONE
LIFE, ONE MIND, ONE BODY, ONE SOUL
TO KNOW HOW PRECIOUS YOU ARE
TO SO MANY PEOPLE, EVEN IF YOU
 ARE PRECIOUS TO JUST ONE,
THAT ONE, BEING THE MOST IMPORTANT,
WHICH IS YOURSELF
YOU MATTER TO ME MORE THAN
YOU COULD EVER UNDERSTAND
I BEG OF YOU NOT TO BECOME A
STATISTIC OR FOLLOWER
OF ANYONE EXCEPT GOD
YOU SEE THE MAYHEM
GIVES THE MEDIA A JOB
THE SYSTEM A REASON TO
SHUT DOWN
PLACES HOPE ON PAUSE
AND THE PANIC BUTTON
CAUSES ALL OF US TO ASSUME A POSITION
HOLLYWOOD MAKES MILLIONS
ANOTHER KID, OR POET ON THE BLOCK
IN THE SOUTH, SLAIN, IS A HERO

AND THE DREAM CONTINUES...
THIS IS NO COMEDY, BUT A BILLION
DOLLAR INDUSTRY, PLAYING US FOR THE FOOL
AND THE SAME MOVIE
 IS REPLAYED EVERY TWENTY
YEARS OR SO...
TURN OFF THE CHANNEL OF HATE
AND TUNE INTO YOU
MAKE YOUR TOMORROW THE BEST EPISODE,
A SAGA, LEAVE A LEGACY
MAKE A VIDEO OR WRITE YOUR OWN LIFE STORY
BREAK GENERATIONAL CURSES
BY STANDING ON THE ROCK BUILT
BEFORE ANY WALL,
ANY OPINIONS, ANY
DIVISION
I LAY DOWN MY ARMOR
BECAUSE NO WEAPON FORMED
AGAINST ME SHALL PROSPER...
GOD IS SO REAL THAT YOU
SPEAK YOUR FATE THROUGH
THE SPIRITUAL TONGUE
HE LOVES ALL PEOPLE,
REGARDLESS OF COLOR, ECONOMIC STATUS,
THE SOUTH STAYS IN POVERTY
BECAUSE WE ARE ALWAYS
AT THE BOTTOM OF WHAT IS LEFT OF
AFTER THE BARREL
ANOTHER CLIP
ONE LESS BLACK MAN STANDING
I WANT YOU TO LIVE AND
BE SMART
BUT MOST IMPORTANTLY,

YOUNG PEOPLE. I URGE YOU
TO BE PRAYED UP...
BECAUSE I DO NOT WANT TO WITNESS
ANOTHER YOUNG GENERATION
FALLING FOR A SET UP FOR ANOTHER
BLACK LIFE BEING LOST...
PROTEST BY SHOWING LOVE
SIT IN UNIVERSITIES AND CLASSROOMS
AND LEARN SOMETHING
START A BUSINESS
GRIND LIKE THERE IS NO TOMORROW
BECAUSE I ASSURE YOU FROM EXPERIENCE
TWENTY YEARS FROM NOW YOUR PRIORITIES
WILL BE WHAT IS FOR DINNER AND WHERE
YOUR NEXT MEAL WILL COME FROM
HOW YOU EAT WILL BE DETERMINED
BY THE COMPANY YOU KEEP IN THE
LONG RUN
SO SURROUND YOURSELF WITH BREADWINNERS
AND POSITIVE PEOPLE WHO DO NOT
NEED OTHERS TO GAIN POWER AND CONTROL
OVER
FEED YOUR MIND, BODY, AND SPIRIT
IF I KNEW THEN, WHAT I KNOW NOW
LIFE IS THE GREATEST TEACHER
SURVIVAL IS PURSUING
YOUR GOALS BY ANY MEANS NECESSARY,
AS LONG AS YOU KEEP PROTOCOL

HERE I AM
TAKE MY HEART
MAKE ME WHOLE AGAIN
I AM YOURS
I COME WITH MY SOUL
POURING OUT TO YOU
WE ARE ONE
I AM AMAZED
BY YOUR LOVE
I WANT TO SING
OF YOUR LOVE
YOU ARE THE ONLY
ONE MY HEART
DREAMS OF
SO, I STAND BEFORE
YOU AND GIVE MYSELF
AWAY
HERE I AM
TAKE THE BROKEN PIECES
AND PUT THEM BACK
TOGETHER AGAIN
HERE I'LL STAND
WAITING TO BE LOVED
AGAIN
I GIVE MYSELF TO YOU
KNOWING THAT ALL
THINGS ARE POSSIBLE
AND YOUR LOVE IS
INFALLIBLE
SO, HERE I AM
WITH YOU I STAND
WAITING ON YOUR PROMISES
MY LOVE

GOD'S MEAL PLAN

DRINK FROM DEEP RIVERS
THAT RUN LONG,
LIKE STORIES TOLD BY ELDERS
SIP FROM FOUNTAINS OF YOUTH,
AND OPEN YOUR MOUTH GAPING WIDE
TO TASTE SHOWERS FROM DARK SKIES
WHEN STORMS COME…
TASTE JOY AND HAPPINESS…
FILL YOUR GLASSES WITH FAITH,
AND HOPE FOR THE BEST…
LET DISAPPOINTMENT DRIBBLE
FROM YOUR LIPS UNTIL IT DISSIPATES…
EAT COURAGE FOR BREAKFAST,
AND HAVE INTEGRITY FOR DESERT…
SNACK ON HUMILITY,
AND DINE WITH HONOR…
SERVE YOURSELF DAILY
DOSES OF LAUGHTER…
AND TRY YOUR BEST,
TO SWALLOW
FORGIVENESS IN SMALL DOSES…
EAT, DRINK, AND BE CONSCIOUS…
SIT AT THE ROUNDTABLE OF COMPASSION
AND PLAN HOW WE CAN FEED THE

HUNGRY, NOURISH THE POOR, AND EDUCATE THE MASSES
FILL YOUR PANTRY WITH UNCONDITIONAL LOVE
ALWAYS KEEP SOUL FOOD ON THE MENU
FEAST ON GOD'S PERFECT MEAL PLAN FOR TWO

MY IDEAL WORLD IS A WHOLE FOODS MARKET

BARBED WIRE
IF IN BARBED WIRE,
FLOWERS BLOOM
AMIDST PURPLE BLUE SKIES...
PICKET FENCES AND CHAINS
CANNOT STOP A SUMMER'S BLOOM
NOR, CAN A BRICK WALL COVET A
GARDEN VIEW...
CONCRETE CANNOT STOP THE TINIEST
FLOWER FROM PEEKING ITS HEAD
TO SUN DANCE IN RAIN
LINES CANNOT CONTOUR THE GROWTH
OF UNEXPECTED BEAUTY
OR THE SHARING
OF THE SEEDS PLANTED
TRELLIS CANNOT CONTAIN THE
WEEDS THAT COMPLIMENT IT
IF IN BARBED WIRE, FLOWERS BLOOM,
WHY CAN'T WE?
WE ARE A GARDEN OF LOVE,
A GARDEN OF HOPE,
A GARDEN OF ONE...
A GARDEN OF UNITY

MY STUFF

YOU SAY YOU ARE LEAVING
AND YOU DON'T WANT ME ANYMORE
THAT'S FINE...
YOU SAY YOU CANNOT FORGIVE ME
FOR WHAT GOD ALLOWED
BUT, BEFORE YOU GO,
TAKE THIS BROWN PAPER BAG
AND PLACE EVERYTHING I GAVE INSIDE
AND GIVE IT BACK...
I WANT EVERY BIT OF MY SUPPORT,
MY UNCONDITIONAL LOVE,
MY MONEY, AND MY HEART...
JUST GIVE ME ALL OF MY SPIRIT,
MY POSITIVE VIBES, BACK RUBS,
AND NOT TO MENTIONS...
MY LOYALTY, MY TRUST,
THE TIMES I CARED FOR YOU,
WHEN YOU WERE SICK OF YOURSELF...
THE TIMES THAT I CRIED WITH YOU
BECAUSE YOU WERE AN EMOTIONAL WRECK...
JUST TAKE THIS BAG AND GIVE BACK
EVERY OUNCE OF MY LOVE, EVERY MOMENT,
AND EVERY MINUTE THAT I SPENT
LOVING YOU...
JUST GATHER IT ALL UP AND SCOOP IT
INTO THIS BAG,
SO THAT WHEN I LEAVE THIS PLACE
I WILL GO WITH WHAT I CAME WITH...
BUT WAIT, THEN AGAIN,
I SHOULD BE JUMPING FOR JOY

BECAUSE CHILDREN WERE BORN,
ENEMIES WERE LEARNED,
SONGS WERE WRITTEN,
LOVE WAS EXPLORED,
HOUSES WERE LIVED IN,
AND NEW POEMS WERE
VOICES UNHEARD BEFORE,
FAITH WAS RESTORED
TO THE POINT THAT MY OLD STUFF
NO LONGER MATTERED TO ME
ANYMORE,
EXCEPT THE LAUGHTER OF MY CHILDREN,
THEIR MORNING KISSES,
THEIR GOODNIGHT HUGS,
HONESTLY, THE ONLY THINGS I
ACHE FOR OCCASIONALLY…
NOSE RUBS AND TICKLING
ONCE MORE, I WATCH YOU
LEAVE…
HOPEFULLY YOU
WILL NOT RETURN…
MY STUFF BELONGS TO
ME…
I PRAY DAILY TO FORGET WHAT YOU TOOK…
BUT, YOU COULD NEVER TOUCH MY SOUL
SO KEEP IT
GOD TOLD ME TO TELL YOU
TO KEEP IT!
EAT IT!
FEED IT
UNTIL IT CHOKES YOU!
IT IS A BURDEN TO WATCH STUFF THAT IS NOT YOURS
GOD BLESS THE CHILD THAT'S GOT HIS OWN…

SPECIAL DEDICATIONS FROM THE AUTHOR...IF THERE ARE STORMS IN YOUR LIFE, WALK THROUGH WITH YOUR HEAD HELD UP HIGH AND WHEN YOU GET TO THE OTHER SIDE, THANK GOD THAT YOU SURVIVED. THIS IS DEDICATED TO MY MOM AND DAD FOR GIVING ME LIFE, AND ALWAYS TELLING ME THAT IT WAS MY OWN, THE LATE MRS. DAISY MASON, FOR CALLING ME "YOUNG GIFTED AND BLACK", AFTER I READ A POEM AT HER HOUSE WHEN I WAS TEN YEARS OLD. SPECIAL THANKS TO ALL MY PEOPLE, ALONI, CHRISTOPHER, LITTLE RENIC, MARY, MY SISTER AND EVERYONE'S ANGEL,TRE, VICTORIA, MICHAEL SPEARS SR.(R.I.P.) AND JR.,MARK "ELI", FOR REMINDING ME THAT A POSITIVE NEEDS A POSITIVE CHARGE, AUNT EDNA, AUNT DOROTHY, SHUG, GREGORY L., DOROTHY, DEVIN, AND KEVIN, ROSEMARY AND RAYFIELD PALMER, RISHA, RAM,ROAN, JENNIFER, KAHLIL, CHARLIE, MS. PATRICIA WILLIAMS, CHERYL, DAPHNE MITCHELL, MICHELLE, AHYAN, JAY, MARVIN JR., SIERRA, MRS ACQUANETTA SPEARS, DELISA, SISTER ANNETTE, TAMMIE JACKSON, ANGELA MILLER, RICKY, DELISA MARCHAND, MARGARET AND WINSTON CAVENDISH, MONTY ROSS, AND SULIMAN AT CAFÉ ISTANBUL, DR. KALTENBAUGH, DR. WELLS, DR. TAYLOR, DR. LACEY, DR. MALIN, DE. BOUIE, MR. AND MRS. GRAY, SONDRA ROBERTS. THE WILLIAMS BROTHERS OF CASH MONEY RECORDS, MY HOMETOWN HEROES, FOR ALWAYS MAKING A DIFFERENCE AND NEVER FORGETTING US, BEING GENEROUS AND GIVING BACK TO THE COMMUNITY AND THE CHILDREN OF N.O. MY FAB ANGEL MIA DUMAS, MY DAUGHTER FROM ANOTHER MOTHER. A SELFLESS, SUPPORTIVE SPIRIT, NATURALLY BEAUTIFUL, INSIDE AND OUT, TELLING ME BY ANY MEANS NECESSARY, WHEN I RANTED, CURSED AND TRULY WANTED TO GIVE UP. FRIENDS, FAMILY, AND SUPPORTERS, KNOW THAT YOU MATTER SO MUCH, AND THIS COULD NOT HAVE BEEN ACCOMPLISHED WITHOUT YOUR SUPPORT AND LOVE. THE

TRUTH HURTS IN A GOOD WAY. WHATEVER PART YOU PLAYED IN MY LIFE, GOOD OR BAD, BIG OR SMALL, KNOW THAT I HAD TO GO THROUGH IT ALL TO BECOME THE WOMAN THAT I AM TODAY. THANK YOU ALL FOR BEING A PART OF MY JOURNEY. LIKE WAYNE, MY LITTLE BRO, PROFOUNDLY STATED, "WHATEVER IT IS YOU DO, JUST DO IT." WELL, I DID IT, AND THIS WAS SO AMAZING! HONESTLY, MY ONLY REGRET IS THAT I DID NOT REALIZE MUCH EARLIER THAT EVERYTHING I NEEDED TO BE A VOICE WAS INSIDE OF MYSELF AND I WAS ALWAYS ON THE RIGHT PATH THAT BROUGHT ME TO THIS PLACE. LIFE IS A JOURNEY FILLED WITH SEASONS. I AM HUMBLY GRATEFUL FOR EVERY EXPERIENCE THAT MADE ME WHO I AM TODAY. THINK FREELY! PEACE, BE BLESSED.

DARLENA MARIE SPEARS
IMANI NATION

www.ingramcontent.com/pod-product-compliance
Lightning Source LLC
Chambersburg PA
CBHW031223090426
42740CB00007B/680